College English 2

Intermediate

KMU CE2 Committee

Keimyung University Press

Contents

UNIT 1-1 About Me

Scan for Audio

Pre-Reading Questions

◆ **Think about the following questions.**

1. Do you play any esports? Which ones?
2. What are the similarities and differences between esports and traditional sports (football, snowboarding, table tennis, etc.)?
3. Should esports be included in global sports competitions such as the Olympics?

VOCABULARY PREVIEW

◆ **Match each word with the correct definition.**

1. chess
2. simulate
3. controversy
4. regime
5. athletic
6. strategic

a. strong disagreement about something among a large group of people
b. of or relating to a general plan that is created to achieve a goal
c. a plan or set of rules to make someone become skilled in a sport
d. a game for two players in which each player moves pieces across a board to trap the other's king
e. to look, feel, or behave like (something)
f. of or relating to sports, games, or exercises

THE FUTURE OF SPORTS

Track 01

Not all sports need a ball. Some are played with a **controller**[1]. Competition in games like *Dota 2*, *Call of Duty*, and *League of Legends* has turned fan following into a fast-growing industry called esports. Esports have many of the characteristics of traditional sports: passionate fans, fierce competition, and star players. Large esports events also bring in large investments. Companies such as the Monster Beverage Corporation and celebrities such as Michael Jordan and Drake are all proud **sponsors**[2] of esports teams. Organizers now hope to raise the status of esports to match that of traditional sports. They want players to be recognized as athletes, and they want to compete at global events such as the Olympics. Yet, despite the growing success of the industry, there is still **controversy** over whether or not esports can be considered **genuine**[3] sports. Critics believe that esports, while competitive, are more similar to games such as **chess** or checkers than sports like football and tennis—requiring brains but not athleticism.

Q **Why do some people believe esports cannot be considered genuine sports?**

If sports are classified only by the amount of physical effort they require, then these critics may have a good argument. But let's not be so quick to judge. Esports players might not have the strongest throwing arms or fastest legs. But they do have certain **athletic** abilities. Video games require strong hand-eye coordination and motor skills. Studies have found that esports players can achieve up to 400 **movements**[4] on a keyboard and mouse per minute. Also, esports players' levels of cortisol (the hormone linked to stress) can rise as high as a Formula 1 driver's.

Q **Underline two examples of the physical effects of playing esports.**

1	**controller**	*n.*	a device or piece of equipment used to operate a machine, vehicle, or system
2	**sponsor**	*n.*	a person or organization that pays the cost of an activity, usually in return for the right to advertise
3	**genuine**	*adj.*	actual, real, or true; not false or fake
4	**movement**	*n.*	the act of moving your body or a part of your body

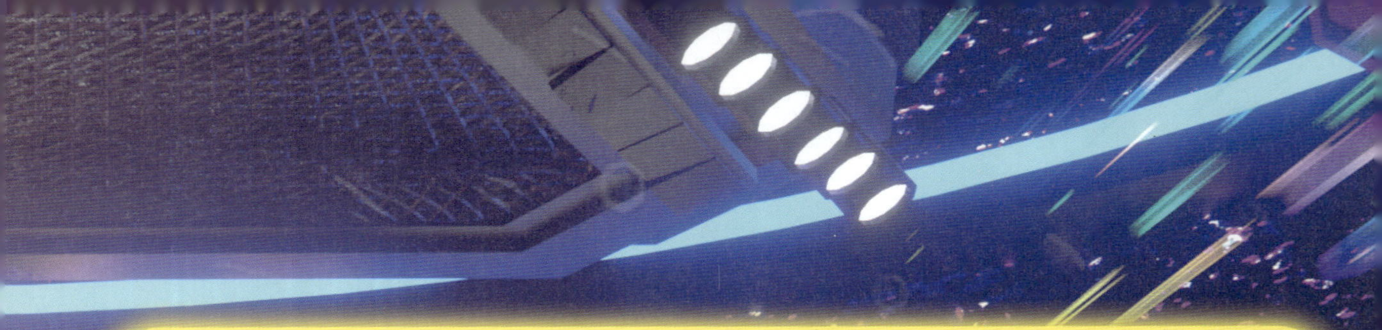

And their heart rates can reach speeds of 160 to 180 beats per minute—a rate **equivalent**[5] to that of someone running at a fast pace.

How do esports teams practice playing under pressure?

Esports players need more than just quick **reflexes**[6]. They also have to have **strategic** minds, **teamwork**[7] and communication skills, and the ability to work under **pressure**[8]. This is why many esports players and teams train like professional athletes and maintain strict training **regimes**. Players will often live with other players or teammates and practice at least eight hours a day. They also have coaches who help by reviewing their past performances, analyzing their competitors' strategies, and coming up with counterstrategies to use in tournaments. Some teams' training sessions even **simulate** esports events. Loud music, cheering fans, and blinding lights are used to distract players and give them practice under pressure.

Esports are already a huge hit. Millions of people tune in to platforms like Twitch and YouTube Gaming every day to watch their favorite players. Tournaments attract studio audiences in the thousands and online **viewers**[9] in the millions. Although there are many who believe esports are not true sports, their preference for physical **excellence**[10] shouldn't prevent esports players from gaining the credit they deserve as professional athletes.

Reading Time: _______ minutes _______ seconds 464 words

5	**equivalent**	*adj.*	having the same value, use, meaning, etc.
6	**reflex**	*n.*	an action or movement of the body that happens automatically as a reaction to something
7	**teamwork**	*n.*	the work done by people who work together as a team to do something
8	**pressure**	*n.*	a feeling of stress or anxiety because people are depending on you for something
9	**viewer**	*n.*	a person who sees or looks at something
10	**excellence**	*n.*	extremely high quality

READING COMPREHENSION

A **Mark each statement as true (T) or false (F) according to the reading.**

1. _____ Famous people and organizations have begun investing in esports.
2. _____ People critical of esports say they're less interesting than "real" sports.
3. _____ Taking part in esports requires little athletic ability.
4. _____ Many serious esports players follow tough training programs.
5. _____ The vast majority of fans watch esports remotely.

B **Choose the best answer according to the reading.**

1. What is the main purpose of the reading? PURPOSE
   a. To describe the profits investors can make from esports
   b. To discuss the differences between traditional sports and esports
   c. To talk about the careers of famous esports athletes
   d. To argue that esports players should be regarded as athletes

2. Which skill or ability do esports players usually NOT have? DETAIL
   a. Strong hand-eye coordination
   b. A strong throwing arm
   c. Quick reflexes
   d. A strategic mind

3. What can be inferred about esports? INFERENCE
   a. Esports have more viewers than traditional sports.
   b. Esports are more physically demanding than traditional sports.
   c. Esports require as much dedication as traditional sports.
   d. Esports require greater communication than traditional sports.

4. In paragraph 4, the phrase *physical excellence* is closest in meaning to ______. VOCABULARY
   a. a strategic mind
   b. a superior body
   c. a competitive attitude
   d. a high cortisol level

C **Fill in the blanks with information from the reading.**

1. Esports teams have a number of celebrity ________________________, including Michael Jordan and Drake.
2. An esports player's ________________________ level and heart rate can reach that of a traditional sports player.
3. Coaches spend a lot of time analyzing players' past ________________________ and competitors' strategies.

SUMMARY

Fill in the blanks with the phrases in the box.

training regimes	similar to games	physical abilities
hand-eye coordination	traditional sports	elevated heart rate

Many people think that esports players should not be considered "athletes." These critics believe that to be an athlete, you must demonstrate 1 ______________________ such as a strong throwing arm. They suggest esports are more 2 ______________________ such as chess than sports such as baseball. However, esports players do have a number of similarities to players of 3 ______________________. They must have strong 4 ______________________ and motor skills. An esports player can also experience a(n) 5 ______________________ and cortisol level, just as players of traditional sports do. Esports players even have coaches and follow strict 6 ______________________ to perfect their strategies and techniques. Maybe esports players are athletes after all.

VOCABULARY PRACTICE

Fill in the blanks with the words in the box. Change the form if necessary.

strategic	regime	simulate	athletic	chess	controversy

1. Derek's ______________________ ability was clear at age five when he started playing soccer.
2. There is ______________________ over whether video games cause violence in real life.
3. Governments have to make ______________________ decisions about their countries' futures.
4. A healthy diet and a strict training ______________________ are a must if you want to play sports professionally.
5. Checkers and ______________________ are two of the oldest board games in the world.
6. Every year, computers are getting better at ______________________ conditions in the real world.

SPEAKING

1A My Personality

A Warm-up

Talk about the questions as a class.

1. Do you know anyone who is an extrovert?
2. Do you know anyone who is an introvert?
3. Do you know anyone who is an ambivert?
4. Which word best describes your personality?

B Authentic Text

1. Read and circle the words that can be used to describe someone's personality. Then answer the questions. Track 02

Paragraph 1

Everyone has a different personality. Some people are lively and social, while others are shy and quiet. Scientists describe people who love being in groups as extroverted. They describe people who prefer to be alone as introverted.

Paragraph 2

Extroverts like being the center of attention and do well in most social situations. They are comfortable at parties and become bored when they are alone. Extroverts communicate well and appear to be friendly, charming, and approachable. These qualities make extroverts excellent salespeople, event planners, financial advisers, and even hairstylists.

Paragraph 3

Often described as loners, introverts prefer spending time engaged in their own interests. Some people believe introverts are never confident, but that belief is not true. Many introverts are more comfortable listening than speaking. Introverts have many other good qualities. They are often more creative than extroverts, and they appear to be calmer and more thoughtful. Suitable careers for introverted people include scientific researchers, artists, photographers, programmers, and accountants.

Paragraph 4

Not everyone's character can be clearly defined as introverted or extroverted. Most people can be one or the other, depending on the situation. For this reason, many scientists argue for a third personality type: ambiverts. Ambiverts are people who can change between introversion and extroversion. They don't hate attention, but they also don't seek it out.

Brief note

The *center of attention* is someone who attracts the attention or interest of everyone in a group.

2. Choose the best title for each paragraph.

_________ I'm a Listener, Not a Talker　　_________ Who I Am

_________ A Little Bit of Both　　_________ Look at Me!

3. Choose the four statements below that are true according to the information in the reading.

1. ☐ People who feel more comfortable in social situations are extroverts.
2. ☐ Introverts are not very friendly.
3. ☐ Extroverts are not creative.
4. ☐ Extroverts make good salespeople.
5. ☐ Introverts are often called loners.
6. ☐ Introverts do not always lack confidence.

C Vocabulary

Put the words in the columns you think they belong in. You can use the words more than once. Discuss your answers as a class.

lively	social	shy	quiet	charming
confident	creative	calm	thoughtful	loner

Introvert	Ambivert	Extrovert

D Use the Language

Who would you like to go traveling with?

1. You have won a free trip to one of the following destinations. Pick a location and two friends to take along. Then write a short description of your friends.

Las Vegas

Lake Tahoe

Aspen

Friend #1

Name: ____________________

Hobbies/Interests:

____

Personality:

____

Friend #2

Name: ____________________

Hobbies/Interests:

____

Personality:

____

2. Answer the questions. Discuss them as a class.

1. Why would you bring Friend #1?

____

2. Why would you bring Friend #2?

____

3. Why did you choose ____________________ as your destination?

____

4. Do you think that your friends will like the destination? Why?

____

____

____

WRITING

1. Write about your first week as a Keimyung University student.

2. What challenges did you have?

3. What did you enjoy most?

SUPPLEMENTAL READING

Racing to Save the Planet

Track 03

Motorsports are exciting for many, but this excitement could be coming at a cost. Many people are starting to question motorsports such as Formula 1, NASCAR, and MotoGP because of their impact on the environment. It's estimated that over 1.8 million kilograms of carbon dioxide are released per year from NASCAR races alone. As people everywhere wake up to the reality of climate change, many are wondering whether motorsports can continue to be justified. But if it's time to turn off the engines, where will fans turn for entertainment?

For car and bike fans, there's an alternative that's far less of a threat to the environment: video games. Racing games are becoming increasingly realistic, making them a practical alternative to real racing. The potential of esports racing was highlighted in 2020 when the COVID-19 pandemic caused the delay or cancellation of several motorsports events. Online racing games experienced a notable increase in viewers as a result.

Of course, there are many reasons why fans will continue to prefer real racing to the digital kind. In particular, the sense of danger in real racing doesn't exist in video games. Drivers' decision-making and abilities vary greatly when you factor in all the conditions they face on real racetracks. People also have to accept that the sound and feel of watching or being in a real race will likely never be fully reproduced in a digital format. But surely, when we think about the health of our planet, there must be room for compromise.

Fill in the blanks with information from the reading.

1. More and more people are realizing the effects ____________________ are having on the environment.
2. Realistic racing games are becoming a(n) ____________________ to racing in the real world.
3. Video games are still not able to fully reproduce the ____________________ faced by drivers in the real world.

EXTENSION Talk or Write About It

Which other sports can be played as both an esport and a physical sport (in real life)? What are the pros and cons of playing these sports in a digital format?

UNIT 1-2 About Me

Scan for Audio

Pre-Reading Questions

◆ **Think about the following questions.**

1. Do you play computer, console, or mobile games? Which types of games do you play?
2. What are the most popular games at the moment? Do you play them?
3. Do you know anyone who is addicted to games? If so, why do you think that person became addicted?

VOCABULARY PREVIEW

◆ **Match each word with the correct definition.**

1. stereotype •
2. productive •
3. portray •
4. niche •
5. incidence •
6. statistic •

- • a. to show or describe someone or something
- • b. how often something happens, especially something bad
- • c. a number that represents a piece of information
- • d. an often unfair and untrue belief that many people have about all people or things with a particular characteristic
- • e. working hard and getting good results
- • f. interesting to, aimed at, or affecting only a small number of people

GAMERS: IMAGE AND REALITY

Track 04

Nearly 50% of gamers are women.

Video games have come a long way since they first **emerged**[1] as a **niche** pastime in the 1970s. In 2020, the global video-game market was worth **approximately**[2] $150 to $160 billion, and it is predicted to continue growing at a rapid pace. Much of this growth is credited to new software and the increasing affordability of mobile devices. According to the Entertainment Software Association (ESA), three out of every four US households include someone who plays video games. Yet, despite the popularity of gaming, there are many negative **stereotypes** attached to being a gamer. This raises the question: how do the stereotypes compare to reality?

Gamers are often **portrayed** negatively in the media. This can be seen in shows such as *The Big Bang Theory*, where the game-obsessed lead characters are noticeably **lacking**[3] in social skills. A common stereotype is that gaming is an activity for boys and young men who lack the energy and motivation to do anything **constructive**[4]. This leads many people to believe that gamers are unhealthy and unlikely to be **productive** because they devote little time to exercise, creative hobbies, and schoolwork. It also leads to fears that young gamers won't be able to hold jobs when they leave school.

As with any group, there are people who fit the stereotypes. However, studies have found that video-game players are far more diverse than we are led to believe. The ESA found in 2018 that gamers primarily consisted of adults, not children. They also found that forty-six percent of gamers were women. Gamers were also not as lazy as some assumed. US unemployment, particularly among young adults in their twenties, steadily declined between 2010 and 2020. Additionally, fifty-six percent of gamers reported that they regularly

Q Underline three pieces of evidence that show stereotypes of gamers are incorrect.

1	**emerge**	*v.*	to become known or apparent
2	**approximately**	*adv.*	almost correct or exact
3	**lacking**	*adj.*	not having any or enough of something that is needed or wanted
4	**constructive**	*adj.*	helping to develop or improve something

participated in creative activities, such as drawing, singing, and writing. Lastly, regarding health, a study at the University of Wurzburg found that only one percent of adult gamers' health problems could be directly linked to gaming and that no **significant**[5] link between games and poor health among children and teenagers existed.

What evidence do researchers give to show that violent games don't lead to real-world violence?

The most serious charge against gamers, however, comes from the belief that games **contribute**[6] to **violence**[7]. High-profile crimes, such as the Sandy Hook **shootings**[8] in the US, have been linked to violent games. Yet, there is no solid evidence connecting video-game violence with real-world violence. In 2020, the American Psychological Association found that violent video games did increase "**aggression**[9]." However, the study pointed out that aggression is not the same as violence. Looking at US crime **statistics**, researchers also found that violent crime, particularly among the young, has decreased since the early 1990s. Additionally, the **incidence** of violent crime in other countries where violent video games are popular is lower than in the US.

Why did people turn to games during the pandemic?

If we look past the stereotypes, we can find that gaming has some positive effects. In 2020, the COVID-19 pandemic led to mass quarantines. People turned to games and social media to relieve their boredom. Games such as *Animal Crossing: New Horizons* became popular topics of social discussion. Rishi Chadha, global head of gaming partnerships at X, noticed the game's impact by tracking conversation volume on X. He found that conversation about the game had grown by over 1,000 percent since its launch, and the number of people posting about the game had increased by over 400 percent. That's more than thirty-eight million posts!

It's easy to find examples that support negative stereotypes about gamers. But **contemporary**[10] research shows gamers are far more complex and diverse than the stereotypes would suggest. Perhaps it's time to reevaluate our image of gamers to better match reality.

Reading Time: _______ minutes _______ seconds 598 words

[5] **significant**	*adj.*	large enough to be noticed or have an effect
[6] **contribute**	*v.*	to help to cause something to happen
[7] **violence**	*n.*	the use of physical force to harm someone, to damage property, etc.
[8] **shooting**	*n.*	an occurrence in which a person is shot with a gun
[9] **aggression**	*n.*	angry or threatening behavior
[10] **contemporary**	*adj.*	happening or beginning now or in recent times

READING COMPREHENSION

A **Mark each statement as true (T) or false (F) according to the reading.**

1. ______ A majority of American households include at least one gamer.
2. ______ The media often portrays gamers as socially confident.
3. ______ More teenage boys play video games than any other group.
4. ______ Experts have found that violent games encourage aggressive behavior.
5. ______ Many people played games on social media during quarantine.

B **Choose the best answer according to the reading.**

1. What is the main purpose of the reading? PURPOSE
   a. To show how the gaming industry has increased in value
   b. To compare the stereotypes and realities of gaming
   c. To describe the growing popularity of mobile gaming
   d. To explain the development of games since the 1970s

2. Which is NOT a stereotype about gamers? DETAIL
   a. Gamers are highly motivated.
   b. The majority of gamers are male.
   c. Gamers tend not to be athletic.
   d. Socializing is difficult for gamers.

3. What can be inferred from paragraph 4? INFERENCE
   a. Violent games are more popular in the US than elsewhere.
   b. Many people believe games are a major cause of violent crime.
   c. The US experiences more crime than other countries.
   d. Violent crime is likely caused by factors other than violent games.

4. The word *its* in paragraph 5 refers to ______. REFERENCE
   a. X
   b. social media
   c. *Animal Crossing: New Horizons*
   d. COVID-19

C **Find the correct numbers in the reading and write them on the lines.**

1. ____________ : the approximate value of the video-game market
2. ____________ : the percentage of gamers that reported participating in creative activities
3. ____________ : the number of posts that talked about Animal Crossing: New Horizons

SUMMARY

Fill in the blanks with the phrases in the box.

range of hobbies	social skills	a negative impact
commit violent acts	large minority	have the energy

Gamers

Image

- Gamers lack 1 ________________.
- The majority of gamers are boys or young men.
- Gamers don't 2 ________________ to do anything constructive with their time.
- Playing games encourages gamers to 3 ________________ in real life.

Reality

- Most gamers are adults, and a 4 ________________ are women.
- The majority of gamers are also productive employees.
- Many gamers have a(n) 5 ________________ and interests.
- Gaming does not have 6 ________________ on the health of young people.

VOCABULARY PRACTICE

Fill in the blanks with the words in the box. Change the form if necessary.

niche	statistic	incidence	portray	stereotype	productive

1. Have you seen the latest employment ________________ for young adults?
2. I wasn't very ________________ this weekend. I just stayed at home and played games.
3. The newspapers have ________________ her as a real hero.
4. The ________________ of cheating in final exams was extremely high.
5. Train watching is a really ________________ hobby.
6. I think you should get to know people rather than relying on ________________.

SPEAKING

1B My Hobbies

A Authentic Text

Read the email. Underline the present perfect and present perfect continuous verbs.

TO:	rjwesley@nmail.com
FROM:	cwesley@ubs.edu
SUBJECT:	Update
DATE:	15 August

Hi, Mom and Dad.

How have you been doing? Sorry I haven't written for a few days. I've been **decorating** my dorm, exploring the campus, and getting to know my roommate. Lucia is really cool—she's into photography. She goes **camping** a lot in the mountains, where she takes photos of the **scenery** and **wildlife**. She also paints. I've seen some of her pictures, and they're beautiful!

We've made plans to go to her favorite **campsite** this Saturday. Two of her friends are coming, too. I told her that I've never been camping before, so she'll have to teach me everything. In exchange, I'm going to teach her about computers. Except for cameras, she knows nothing about **electronics**! I'm going to help her set up a **blog** so she can **upload** her nature photos and other **artwork**.

This afternoon, Lucia and I are going shopping for some new camping **equipment**. I'll tell you all about the trip on Monday.

Love,

Christine

Brief note

The phrase *in exchange* means that "one thing is given for another," or "one favor is done for another."

B Vocabulary

Write the words in bold from the reading next to the correct definition. Some words will not be used.

1. ____________ making (something) more attractive by putting something on it
2. ____________ the activity of sleeping outdoors in a tent, usually for fun
3. ____________ to move or copy (a file, program, etc.) from a storage device to a larger computer or network
4. ____________ a website on which a person or group posts new information regularly
5. ____________ a view of natural surroundings that is pleasing to look at
6. ____________ supplies or tools needed for a special purpose

C In Your World

Types of Hobbies

Look over the categories. Each student will take turns naming a hobby or thing that fits in each category. When students run out of ideas (or when someone repeats an idea), move on to the next category. Take notes on new vocabulary on a separate sheet of paper.

1. The Arts	2. Musical Instruments	3. Nature/The Outdoors	4. Sports/Physical Activities	5. Games
painting,	*guitar,*	*camping,*	*jogging,*	*chess,*

D Grammar

Present perfect tense

simple present vs. present continuous			
simple present		**present continuous**	
routine actions or habits	She **paints**.	actions now	They're **sitting** in class.
facts	Electronics **are** expensive.	temporary facts	I'**m living** in the dorm this year.
		future plans	We'**re going** shopping later.
present perfect			
past states/actions continuing to the present	I'**ve been** a teacher since 2015. How long **have** you **worked** here?	completed actions	I'**ve finished** my homework, so now I can relax.
experiences	**Has** he ever **been** camping?	recent events; news	We'**ve made** plans for the weekend.
present perfect continuous			
ongoing actions, not finished		They'**ve been living** in this building for a year. (They still do.)	
actions that were ongoing and have finished		I'**ve been exploring the campus** all day. (I'm tired. I'm going to bed.)	

1. Match the sentences with their correct tenses and functions.

1. I've been jogging for an hour. Now I need a shower. •
2. There is interesting wildlife in these mountains. •
3. We're taking a photography class this semester. •
4. Ellen's been sleeping for a long time. Should we wake her up? •

• a. present perfect continuous: finished action
• b. present perfect continuous: not finished
• c. present continuous: temporary facts
• d. simple present: fact

2. **Underline the mistake and write the corrections on the line. If the sentence is correct, write OK.**

action verbs vs. stative verbs	
Action verbs describe actions and can be used in continuous tenses.	eat, play, watch, drive, work, tell, sleep, shop, write, go, laugh, etc.
Stative verbs describe states and are not usually used in continuous tenses.	be, seem, remember, understand, know, own, like, love, hate, forget, etc.

1. I'm sorry, but I'm not understanding. ______________________
2. We're staying in a hotel until July 15. ______________________
3. Julia has been liking chess since she was a kid. ______________________
4. You've been working too hard lately. ______________________

E Use the Language

Hobby Guessing Game

1. **Fill out the chart. Choose a partner. Take turns guessing each other's hobbies. Do not show your partner your chart.**

	My Responses	My Partner's Responses (Guess!)
A hobby I've done for a long time		
A hobby I tried but didn't enjoy		
A hobby I'd like to try in the future		
A hobby I will never try		

2. **Share your table with your partner. How good were your guesses? Discuss the reasons for your choices.**

WRITING

1. What do you like to do when you have free time?

2. Have you joined any school clubs since you came to Keimyung University?

SUPPLEMENTAL READING

Are Gamers Good Students?

Track 05

For decades parents have complained that video games distract children from their schoolwork and harm their academic performance. But is there any evidence that this is actually true? Scientists have conducted a number of studies that should help lay concerned parents' fears to rest.

One common theory is that gamers devote less time to academic activities than non-gamers. Therefore, their academic performance is likely to be worse than that of non-gamers. Studies that tested this idea found that gamers did spend less time on their homework than non-gamers. However, they also found that the academic performance of the two groups was similar. Some researchers even think that games can actually improve academic performance. These researchers suggest that video games can improve students' visual awareness, memory, and attention capacity, and can train students to think critically.

Recent studies have strengthened the argument that games have little negative effect on academic performance. A team of German researchers conducted a study of students across their entire school career. As a part of the study, they monitored their video-game usage. Approximately seventy percent of the students in the study played video games occasionally. Of them, twenty percent spent two or more hours daily playing games. The team concluded that students who played games for long periods of time did get worse grades overall. Yet when tested on their understanding of core math and language concepts, heavy gamers performed well, suggesting that gaming has no significant effect on overall learning.

It seems that, within reason, gaming does not harm students' academic potential. They just need to remember to put their controllers aside from time to time.

Fill in the blanks with information from the reading.

1. ______________________________ spend more time on their homework than gamers do.
2. One study found that the ______________________________ of both gamers and non-gamers was similar.
3. Around ______________________________ of the students in the German study played games occasionally.

EXTENSION Talk or Write About It

Overall, do you think playing computer, console, or mobile games is a good way to spend your free time? Why or why not?

UNIT 2-1 Memories

Scan for Audio

Pre-Reading Questions

◆ **Think about the following questions.**

1. Can you name a time when you had trouble remembering something important?
2. Can you name some parts of the brain that you know? What do they do?
3. Do you think it is possible to improve your memory? How might someone do this?

VOCABULARY PREVIEW

◆ **Read the definitions. Then match each word in bold with its definition.**

A. lasting forever
B. damage to someone's body caused by an accident or attack
C. to come from or originate
D. a thin thread in the body that carries messages between the brain and other parts of the body

1. ________ **Injuries** interfere with the brain's normal working processes.
2. ________ Sometimes brain damage can be **permanent**.
3. ________ Damaged **nerve** cells cannot send information the way they need to.
4. ________ What we know about the brain **stems** from past studies of brain injuries.

What Brain Injuries Teach Us about Memory

Track 06

The brain is the control center for all of our activities. Brain injuries interfere with its normal working processes. Injury damages nerve cells, and then they cannot send information in an effective way. Scientists learn a lot by studying brain injuries, and they have particularly learned a lot about memory this way.

Scientists first studied the brain by looking into injuries to it. During World War I, many soldiers suffered brain injuries. By studying injured brains, scientists saw that injuries in the same regions usually caused the same symptoms. They used this information to create maps of brain regions and their functions. Much of what we know about the brain today stems from this study of brain injuries.

A healthy brain works like a computer. It takes in, stores, and later retrieves information. A new memory is first stored as a short-term one. The important information is then moved to another area and stored as long-term memory. The more this information is accessed, the more likely it will stay in long-term memory. These memories last for years.

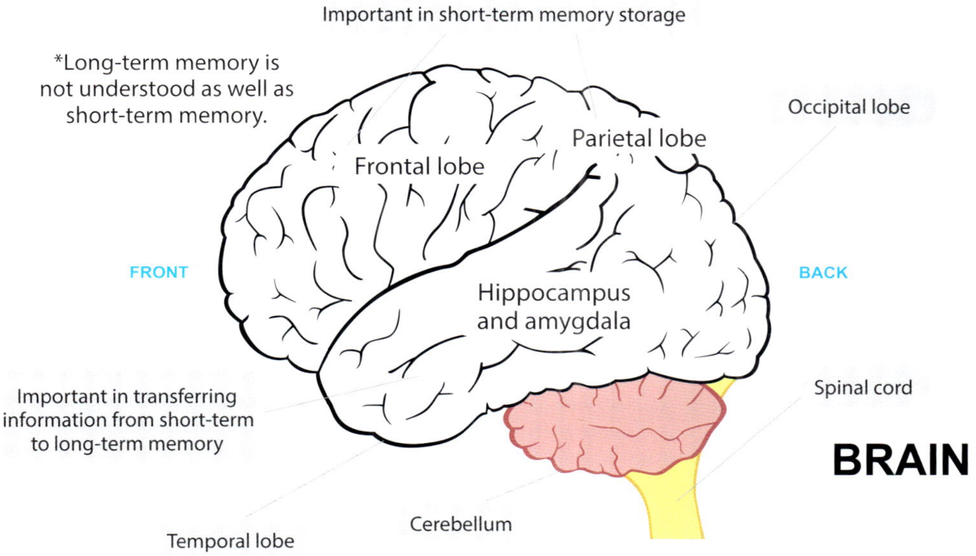

▲ Memory and regions of the brain

An injured brain can have trouble with long-term memory. Injured people are unable to recall the past and sometimes can't even remember their own names. Problems with short-term memory are much more common, however, and since short-term memories are the building blocks for long-term ones, both are affected. Once a person suffers a head injury that affects short-term memory, the person will have difficulty creating new long-term memories. The effects are amazing. A person whose brain was recently injured can talk about memories from 15 years ago but often not about things that happened 15 minutes ago.

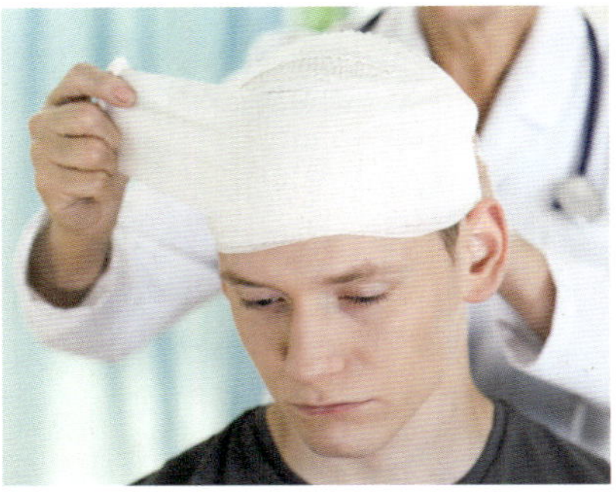

▲ Brain injuries can cause memory loss.

To review, then, memory is complex and it is often affected by head trauma. Short-term and long-term memories can both be affected, and sometimes the damage can be permanent. Fortunately, many injuries heal over time. As scientists learn more, they will become better able to contribute to the healing process.

Reading Time: _______ minutes _______ seconds 324 words

Review the Highlights

◆ **Mark up the text and infographic according to the instructions.**

1. Look at Paragraph 1. Paraphrase the thesis sentence. ______________________________
____
2. Look at Paragraph 2. Underline how World War I helped scientists.
3. Look at Paragraph 3. Put stars next to what computers and brains do with information.
4. Look at Paragraph 4. Underline the sentences about how short-term memory affects long-term memory.
5. Look at Paragraph 5. Put a star next to what happens to many head injuries.
6. Look at the infographic. Circle the sentence about long-term memory.

READING COMPREHENSION

A **Circle the correct answer.**

1. Why does the author refer to the brain as "the control center"? Details: why
   a. Because it is in the center of the body
   b. Because it controls the body
   c. Because the body controls it
   d. Because it works the hardest

2. What did scientists learn during World War I? Details: what
   a. They learned how to memorize maps for war.
   b. They learned the soldiers' functions by studying their brains.
   c. They learned about the brain from soldiers with brain injuries.
   d. They learned how brain injuries occur.

3. According to Paragraph 3, what can our brains do with memories? Details: what
   a. Take them in, change them, and store them
   b. Store them, retrieve them, and change them
   c. Make them up, store them, and change them
   d. Take them in, store them, and retrieve them

4. Which sentence is NOT supported by the text? Negative fact
   a. Injured brains can have trouble with short-term or long-term memory.
   b. Injured brains usually have more problems with short-term memory.
   c. If short-term memory is affected, long-term memory will also be affected.
   d. If long-term memory is affected, short-term memory will also be affected.

5. What can be inferred from the reading? Inference
   a. There is still much to learn about the brain and how it works.
   b. Most people never recover from brain injuries.
   c. The brain controls when and where it is injured.
   d. The brain has a difficult time holding onto memories.

B **Complete the summary. Write the words from the reading that best fit in the blanks. One word is extra.**

stems recall cell injuries fortunately nerve permanent functions

Much of what we know about the brain 1. ______________ from studies of injured brains. These studies helped scientists create maps of brain regions and their 2. ______________. They also taught scientists that brain 3. ______________ damage 4. ______________ cells, which affects memory. This damage can affect long-term memory, making people unable to 5. ______________ the past. Or it might damage short-term memory, so that people cannot create new memories. 6. ______________, the damage is not always 7. ______________. Many brain injuries heal over time.

SUMMARY

1. **Listen to the conversation and take notes on the memorization tips.** Track 07

Helpful Tips for Memorization

1.	2.	3.	4.

2. **Work with a partner. Talk about memorization, and take notes on what your partner says. Make sure to answer the questions below as you talk.**

How do you memorize things?
What types of things are difficult for you to memorize? (people's names, numbers, facts, etc.)
What types of things are easy for you to memorize?
What tips do you know for memorization?
What advice have teachers given you in the past for memorizing things?
Is it easiest for you to remember things you see, things you hear, or things you read? Why?
How do you think people can improve their memories?

Notes

3. **Write a paragraph about improving memorization. Include tips that might be helpful to students. Then share your paragraph with your classmates.**

____

____

VOCABULARY PRACTICE

Fill in the blanks with the words in the box. Change the form if necessary.

interfere	symptom	retrieve	affect	trauma

1. Some COVID-19 patients have common flu ____________________.
2. How can I ____________________ information from the database?
3. Survivors from the World War II expressed their shared ____________________.
4. I am deeply ____________________ by the film *Parasite* by Bong Joon-ho.
5. Please do not ____________________ in my work.

SPEAKING

2A What I Miss

A Warm-up

Talk about the questions as a class.

1. Describe a good childhood memory.
2. What TV shows do you miss from your childhood?
3. What foods do you miss from your childhood?
4. What fashion trends do you miss from your childhood?

B Authentic Text

1. Read the article and underline sentences written in the past tense. Then answer the questions. Track 08

WHY THE LATE 90S WERE THE BEST TIME TO GROW UP

Brief note

Can't help but ~ is used to say that someone is unable to choose any but one kind of action.

By: Amy Anderson

Paragraph 1

Do you know what nostalgia is? Nostalgia is that feeling of both happiness and sadness that you get when thinking about something in your past. Just about anything can cause this feeling: a smell, a sound, or an image. The other day, I was looking through an old yearbook and felt very nostalgic. That made me stop and think about what I miss most about my childhood.

Paragraph 2

Every generation grows up with different celebrities and musicians. When I was a teenager, pop music consisted of boy bands like NSYNC, idol singers like Britney Spears, and hip-hop stars like Jay Z. Of course, there were also many other different types of music. But these artists dominated the charts and radio. Even now, when I hear the start of the song "Still D.R.E," I can't help but dance.

Paragraph 3

Food trends don't change as often as celebrity trends. But there are a lot of foods from my childhood that I miss. For example, I had a sweet, cookie-flavored cereal every morning while I was watching cartoons. The company stopped making that cereal years ago. Maybe that's because it wasn't very healthy. Or maybe it died out because people became more conscious of what they and their kids eat. Whatever the reason, I feel a little sad when I realize that I can never have my favorite cereal again.

Paragraph 4

Another thing that I miss about my youth is the clothes. Fashion trends always seem to come and go quickly. For example, when I was a teenager, people were bleaching their hair tips, wearing popped collars on polo shirts, and buying Starter jackets. Those things stopped being fashionable a while ago, but I smile when I see them in old photos. I'm still holding on to the hope that one day my Chicago Bulls Starter jacket will come back into style.

2. **Choose the best title for each paragraph.**

__________ I Don't Wanna Grow Up   __________ Please Don't Stop the Music

__________ I Miss that Cereal   __________ Trends Come and Go

3. **Choose the four statements from below that are true according to the information in the reading.**

1. ☐ Nostalgia is a feeling of regret.

2. ☐ NSYNC was a popular boy band.

3. ☐ Food trends change rapidly.

4. ☐ The author's favorite cereal from childhood is no longer available.

5. ☐ Many people changed their hair color when the author was young.

6. ☐ The author still has a jacket that was fashionable in the past.

C Vocabulary

Fill in the blanks with the correct words from the box.

past	childhood	generation	celebrity	trend
style	nostalgic	conscious	died out	hope

1. My sister used to wear her hair in a ponytail on the side of her head because it was a(n) ______________.
2. People have described my ______________ as sophisticated because I wear lots of sports coats.
3. My old friends and I played basketball this weekend, which made me feel ______________.
4. Older people say that people in my ______________ are entitled and lazy, but I disagree.
5. My professor said that, in the ______________, research was more difficult to do because they didn't have the Internet.
6. What I remember most about my ______________ are the cartoons and video games.
7. She was a huge ______________ when I was younger, but I don't see her on television anymore.
8. I used to eat fast food four or five times a week, but now I have to be more ______________ of my diet.
9. There's always ______________, so have a positive attitude about everything you do.
10. I'm glad that the baggy clothes trend ______________. I looked terrible in that stuff!

D Use the Language

Word Association

Play a word game with the class. Your teacher will write a vocabulary word on the board. The first student must read the first word on the board and say/write an "associated" word. Continue until you reach 20 words.

Example: Trend > Fashion > Hip-hop > Eminem > *8 Mile* > Movies > Celebrities > Etc.

ROUND 1

ROUND 2

MEMO

WRITING

1. Write about your favorite childhood memory.

SUPPLEMENTAL READING

The Shattucks: Practitioners of Sharing and Giving

Track 09

Sidney F. Shattuck (1878-1976) was born on April 28, 1878, in Neenah, Wisconsin, USA. He was the eldest son of Franklyn Shattuck, one of the founders of the global paper company Kimberly-Clark, and Clara Shattuck. Sidney Shattuck graduated from Yale University in June 1899 and married Ruth Harwood in 1908. He instilled his lifelong belief in charity in his children. When his children turned seven, Shattuck gave them a weekly allowance of 10 cents, teaching them to allocate 2 cents for savings, 3 cents for charity, and the rest for spending.

In January 1900, Shattuck joined Kimberly-Clark and worked there for 45 years until his retirement in 1945. He worked to establish various welfare systems that were unprecedented at the time. He organized the Kimberly-Clark Mutual Benefit Association, which laid the foundation for modern labor unions. He also created a group insurance system, and in 1913, set up an organization to prevent industrial accidents. In recognition of these achievements, he received an award from the National Safety Council of the United States. Throughout his life, Shattuck donated to numerous charitable causes. Notably, he took over the Neenah-Menasha Boys' Brigade and dedicated his life to volunteer work. In 1964, the Brigade founded the "S.F. Shattuck Award" in honor of his contributions.

In the early 1960s, the Shattucks donated approximately $100,000 to Keimyung University. Today, several commemorative buildings at Keimyung University bear the Shattuck name.

Source: 빛을 여는 계명인. 계명대학교 출판부. 2024, p. 158–161.

EXTENSION Talk or Write About It

1. Do you participate in any volunteer work? If not, would you consider it?
2. What do you know about philanthropy?
3. Do you know any famous philanthropists?

UNIT 2-2 Memories

Scan for Audio

Pre-Reading Questions

◆ **Think about the following questions.**

1. How often do you use the Internet to look up facts you are just curious about?
2. Have you ever been certain of a fact, only to find out you were wrong after looking it up on the Internet?
3. Are you concerned about how much time you spend on the Internet? Why or why not?

VOCABULARY PREVIEW

◆ **Match each word with the correct definition.**

1. faculty •	• a. a specific mental ability
2. impact •	• b. logical soundness
3. static •	• c. effect
4. cognitive •	• d. showing little or no change
5. validity •	• e. negative
6. adverse •	• f. of or relating to mental functioning

IS THE INTERNET RUINING YOUR MEMORY?

Track 10

A prominent educator once warned that a popular new technology was becoming a **crutch**[1], with a negative **impact** on his students' memories. That educator was Socrates, and the new technology he disliked was writing—on wax tablets and papyrus scrolls, to be exact. The great **orators**[2] of his time delivered memorized speeches without notes. Socrates saw writing as a threat to that tradition, and by extension, those mental **faculties**. Or so reported his student Plato in *Phaedrus*, anyway. True to his word, Socrates himself **stubbornly**[3] refused to write his thoughts down.

It's no great leap, therefore, to suppose Socrates would similarly disapprove of the Internet today. His attitude is echoed in growing concerns that the Internet is changing our brains. Many of these concerns center on the so-called "Google effect," which is believed by some researchers and a growing number of journalists to have an **adverse** effect on our memories.

Q Underline the author's guess about how Socrates would view the Internet today.

At the heart of specific concerns about memory is a study authored by psychologist Betsy Sparrow. It was published in 2011 as "Google Effects on Memory" in the journal *Science*. In experiments at Harvard University, Sparrow's team found that subjects exposed to detailed, **trivial**[4] information were more likely to forget it if told they could look it up online later. Subjects also tended to include the Internet among their own **cognitive** tools. It was as if the computer were part of their intellectual abilities. Hence, Sparrow concluded, the Internet has become a central player in our "transactive memory." This is the sharing of information **retention**[5] among persons—or in this case, digital networks—in a group. In short, Google has become everyone's brainy friend, the "walking encyclopedia." Sparrow hypothesized this may have far-reaching effects on the way we think and perhaps even the physiology of our brains.

Q What is transactive memory?

Critics of the study and of many of the other "Google effect" articles

1	**crutch**	*n.*	something that a person uses too much for help or support
2	**orator**	*n.*	a skilled speaker
3	**stubbornly**	*adv.*	in a way that shows no willingness to change one's mind; persistent
4	**trivial**	*adj.*	ordinary; not important
5	**retention**	*n.*	the act of holding on to something; keeping

that followed it point out what they see as significant **flaws**[6]. The first is the questionable **validity** of the assumption that forgetting something because we can google it later is any different from forgetting a phone number immediately after writing it down. The same study showed that frequent Internet users were **adept**[7] at remembering where to find information, if not the information itself. Moreover, Sparrow herself admits that transactive memory is nothing new. Long before Google, we had libraries with librarians and card catalogs to direct our searches.

Is there proof that our memories are, in fact, getting worse because of Internet search engines or that relying on them rather than the library has demonstrable physiological effects? So far, cognitive neuroscience has revealed no such data. And in the US, a country with one of the highest Internet usage rates, average IQ scores continue to steadily rise three points per decade. Standard tests of IQ measure fluid working memory and long-term retention. It may be too soon for a quantifiable negative effect to emerge, but until it does, the **sticklers**[8] for evidence will likely remain unconvinced. "Such panics often fail basic reality checks," the Harvard University research psychologist Steven Pinker states in a *New York Times* article on the subject. "The effects of consuming electronic media are … likely to be far more limited than the panic implies."

What is plasticity?

What we do know about the plasticity—or changeability—of human memory should make us think twice about placing it in such high esteem. Recent findings in neuroscience have proven that we alter memories every time we access them. Therefore, even the most accurate memory is subject to plasticity; over time, connected memories will change each other. This highlights the difference between accessibility and accuracy: some humans may recall information well, but plasticity will affect the accuracy of that information over time. The Internet, by contrast, is not subject to plasticity. That does not mean the information is **static**, however. It's constantly being fact-checked and updated, with a **cumulative**[9] effect that's mostly positive, low-quality online content **notwithstanding**[10].

There may be sociological consequences of Google's power as the main "keeper" of information. But Internet users aren't really consulting Google. They're using it as a tool to access the same scientific journals and respected news sources they might find in the library—if they had all sorts of spare time.

Reading Time: _______ minutes _______ seconds 705 words

6	**flaw**	*n.*	an imperfection
7	**adept**	*adj.*	skilled
8	**stickler**	*n.*	a person who believes that something is important and should always be done or followed
9	**cumulative**	*adj.*	increasing over time through addition
10	**notwithstanding**	*adv.*	in spite of what has just been said

READING COMPREHENSION

A **Mark each statement as true (T) or false (F) according to the reading.**

1. _____ Socrates wrote about his dislike of writing in *Phaedrus*.
2. _____ Sparrow's team found that subjects forgot things they knew they could look up.
3. _____ The Harvard study proved that the Internet changes our brain physiology.
4. _____ Steven Pinker does not believe the Internet is a serious threat to human intelligence.
5. _____ You can alter a memory simply by remembering it.

B **Choose the best answer according to the reading.**

1. What is the main idea of the reading? MAIN IDEA
   a. Reports that the Internet changes memory function may be misleading.
   b. Every new technology has critics who believe it will be bad for humanity.
   c. Internet search engines give us an exaggerated idea of our intelligence.
   d. The Internet has reduced memory capacity, but neuroscientists do not know why.

2. Which is NOT true of Steven Pinker? DETAIL
   a. He is a research psychologist.
   b. He is a reporter for the New York Times.
   c. He is associated with Harvard University.
   d. He is skeptical of claims about electronic media.

3. What is paragraph 6 mainly about? TOPIC
   a. The history of the Internet as a research tool
   b. The reasons our brains can retain long-term memories
   c. An argument in favor of replacing libraries with the Internet
   d. The limitations of human memory compared to the Internet

4. Which statement would the writer most likely agree with? INFERENCE
   a. Low-quality content should be removed from websites.
   b. Google is likely having a positive effect on our memories.
   c. The use of search engines should not be allowed in schools.
   d. The benefits of Google as a tool outweigh its downsides.

C **Fill in the blanks with information from the reading.**

1. Socrates thought that ______________________________ weakened people's minds.
2. The "______________________________" refers to the supposed impact of Internet search engines on our memory.
3. Average IQ scores in the US have been rising by ______________________________ per decade.

SUMMARY

Fill in the blanks with the phrases in the box.

to forget information	ability to remember	Internet's effects
the average IQ	less accurate	our transactive memory

Just as Socrates objected to writing, some people are concerned about the 1 ____________________ on our minds—specifically, our memory. Much of this concern stems from a study that found that subjects were more likely 2 ____________________ if they were told they could look it up online later. The study's author concluded we have integrated the Internet into 3 ____________________, and this may affect our thinking and the makeup of our brains. But some people point out that forgetting something because we can look it up later does not necessarily show a decrease in the 4 ____________________. And if relying on the Internet is bad, isn't relying on the library bad, too? 5 ____________________, which measures memory among other abilities, has been rising steadily in the US. Regardless of the criticism, the Internet has an advantage over human memory, since our memories actually become 6 ____________________ over time. Information on the Internet does not change in this way.

VOCABULARY PRACTICE

Fill in the blanks with the words in the box. Change the form if necessary.

adverse	cognitive	static	faculty	impact	validity

1. Humans have a(n) ________________ for solving problems that other animals do not share.
2. Living languages are never ________________; they are constantly changing.
3. The ________________ of WWII is felt in geopolitics to this day.
4. IQ tests were designed to measure ________________ ability, not general knowledge.
5 Most scientists agree that human activity is having a(n) ________________ effect on the climate.
6 Many of Sigmund Freud's theories remain popular in spite of their lack of scientific ________________.

SPEAKING

2B A Day to Remember

A Authentic Text

Read the essay about the writer's earliest memory. Underline the past perfect and past perfect continuous verbs.

Brief note

To this day means "from then until the present; ever since."

My Earliest Memory

My earliest **memory** from childhood is of my first day of school. I was 5 years old, and I remember it well because it was such an **emotional** day.

I had not been looking forward to starting kindergarten. My parents had told me not to worry and that it was going to be fun. "You'll meet new kids and learn a lot," they'd said. I wasn't **convinced**. School sounded hard and **scary**, and I preferred playing outside with my friends.

That morning, I put on my favorite jeans and T-shirt, which my mom had washed and ironed the night before. My dad served me my favorite cereal for breakfast, too. **Nevertheless**, I felt **miserable**. My mom walked me to school. By the time we got there, I had started crying. (There's a photo of that **moment**, and it makes me laugh to this day.) As we said goodbye, my mom tried to **encourage** me. "Be **brave**," she said. "You can do it."

Of course, my mom was right. My best friend Lena was in my class, and we sat together. Lena and I made some new friends, too. Our teacher taught us games and made funny jokes. At the end of the day, I actually felt **cheerful**. I **realized** that I'd been enjoying myself!

When it was time to go home, my mom met me outside the school. I asked her, "I can come back here tomorrow, can't I?"

B Vocabulary

1. **Write the words in bold from the reading next to the correct definitions. Some words will not be used.**

1. ______________ something that you remember
2. ______________ having or causing a feeling such as happiness or sadness
3. ______________ completely sure
4. ______________ a specific point in time
5. ______________ became aware of; understood
6. ______________ likely to make someone feel frightened
7. ______________ to make someone feel more hopeful or confident

2 **Write the words from the box under the correct pictures.**

brave	jealous	embarrassed	exhausted	cheerful

1. ____________ **2.** ____________ **3.** ____________ **4.** ____________ **5.** ____________

3 **Match the underlined descriptions of feelings with the correct words.**

1. Long, cold, gray winters make some people feel extremely unhappy. •
2. Marco was amazed and could hardly believe it when he saw his friend on TV. •
3. We are very eager to find out more about the new student in our class. •
4. When I didn't get into that university, I was unpleasantly surprised. •

• a. disappointed
• b. miserable
• c. curious
• d. shocked

C About You

Early Memories

Discuss the following questions with a partner.

1. What is your earliest memory? **2.** Do you remember your first day of school? How did you feel?

D Grammar

Past perfect and Past perfect continuous

past perfect	
The past perfect tense is used to talk about an action that was finished before something else happened in the past. It is formed with *had* + past participle.	
an action that happened before a specific time	I arrived at school at 8:25. → At/By 8:30, I **had** (already) **arrived** at school.
	He finished his work Friday morning. → By Friday afternoon, he **had** (already) **finished** his work.
an action that happened before another past action/event	My mom washed and ironed my clothes last night. Then, this morning, I put them on. → This morning, I put on my clothes. My mom **had** (already) **washed** and **ironed** them.
past perfect continuous	
The past perfect continuous is similar to the present perfect continuous, except that the action both began and ended in the past. Use the continuous form when the ongoing action or process is more important than the finished result. It is formed with *had been* + present participle (*-ing*).	
an ongoing action that began and ended in the past	I'm starting school today. I haven't been looking forward to it. → I started school yesterday. I **hadn't been looking** forward to it.
	Now I realize that I've been enjoying myself! → Then I realized that I'**d been enjoying** myself!

1 Circle the correct words.

1. Before his first day of school, my brother had (learned / learning) to read.
2. By 9:00 p.m. last night, Haley (has / had) already gone to bed.
3. We were disappointed because we'd been (hoped / hoping) to see you before you left.
4. When I got home, my feet hurt because I (have / had) been walking all day.

2 Fill in the blanks with the correct forms of the given verbs. Use the present perfect continuous or the past perfect continuous.

1. I was curious to meet Nicole because I ____________________ so much about her. (hear)
2. His girlfriend ____________________ to another guy for a long time, so he felt a little jealous. (talk)
3. Julia's eyes are red. I think she ____________________. (cry)
4. Sam sang the song perfectly at the concert last week. She ____________________ it for a month. (practice)

E Use the Language

Brief note

To *snore* means to make noise through your nose and mouth while you're sleeping.

Memorable Moments

1. Read about a person's most embarrassing moment. Put the story in order from 1 to 7.

____ It was the first class of the morning, and I was exhausted.

____ I realized that I had been sleeping and snoring! Since then, I've never fallen asleep in class again.

____ "Sorry to wake you," the teacher said, "but you were making a lot of noise." The whole class laughed.

____ So, even though I was really trying to listen to the lecture, my eyes kept closing.

__1__ My most embarrassing moment happened in high school when I was in history class.

____ That's because I had stayed up late the night before, watching movies.

____ Then, suddenly, the teacher was calling my name and tapping me on the shoulder. I opened my eyes.

2. Choose one of the following topics. On a separate sheet of paper, write a paragraph about that memory (six to eight sentences). Share your paragraph with the class.

my most embarrassing moment	my bravest moment
my happiest day	my most miserable day

WRITING

1. What was your most memorable day?

2. What did you learn from that experience?

The Inventor of Internet Addiction?

Track 11

Dr. Ivan K. Goldberg, a psychiatrist and clinical psychopharmacologist, came up with the term "Internet addiction" in 1995. But he never thought anyone would take him seriously. In fact, he said the disorder didn't really exist. In 1986, Goldberg created an online club for psychiatrists called PsyCom.net and often browsed the site for news and messages. While reading the messages posted on the site's bulletin boards, he came up with the idea of posting a message to poke fun at the DSM (Diagnostic and Statistical Manual of Mental Disorders), the American Psychiatric Association's definitive list of accepted disorders.

Dr. Goldberg made up a disease called "Internet Addiction Disorder" (IAD). In the message, he described the symptoms of the disease. One symptom was that "important social and occupational activities are given up or reduced because of Internet use." Other symptoms included dreaming about the Internet and having uncontrolled movements of the fingers, as if typing.

To Goldberg's surprise, several colleagues admitted to suffering from IAD and asked him for help. In response, Goldberg set up the Internet Addiction Support Group online for his colleagues. Soon, hundreds of self-described addicts began to post messages on the site, and some people admitted surfing up to twelve hours per day. Several universities and hospitals in the United States began to set up counseling services for those with IAD.

Despite his uneasiness over the part he played in this "discovery," Goldberg posted a message to members of the Internet addicts forum every six months or so until his death in 2013. He tried to get them to examine why they are online so much—and to consider psychotherapy.

Fill in the blanks with information from the reading.

1. In 1995, Dr. Ivan Goldberg invented the term called ______________________.
2. Some of Dr. Goldberg's colleagues asked him ______________________.
3. Dr. Goldberg told Internet addicts that maybe they should try ______________________.

EXTENSION Talk or Write About It

Imagine you had to give up the Internet for an entire year. How would your life change? Would the changes be mostly positive or mostly negative?

UNIT 3-1 Going Out

Scan for Audio

Pre-Reading Questions

◆ **Talk about these questions with your classmates.**

1. What do you know about the animals in the picture?
2. What courting rituals have you seen, on TV or in real life, between animals?
3. What strange courting rituals do you know about?

VOCABULARY PREVIEW

◆ **Read the definition. Then match each word in bold with its definition.**

A. to cry out in a loud and high voice because of pain, surprise, anger, etc.
B. a series of acts that are always performed in the same way
C. a child or animal born to a particular parent
D. to make someone or something want to come to you
E. direct; simple

1. ______ **Offspring** usually stay very close to their mother after birth.
2. ______ Some animals perform courting **rituals** so that they can attract a partner.
3. ______ Some male birds dance to **lure** the female to them.
4. ______ If a female porcupine **screams**, it means that she is not interested in the male.
5. ______ In spite of evolution, mating in the animal kingdom is not a very **straightforward** process.

Strange Love

Track 12

Animals mate to produce offspring so that their genes are passed along. Due to their need to reproduce, it seems like finding a mating partner should be a straightforward process. Actually, though, many animals have to resort to tactics or tricks to find a partner. Some animals stand out because they look unique, while others perform dramatic rituals to woo a mate.

In the animal kingdom, there are many different courting rituals. For example, male bowerbirds are fairly romantic, creating a colorful bower, or an attractive shelter, for their future mate. The female chooses her mate based on the beauty of his bower. The male bowerbird will also dance for the female in an attempt to attract her. Similarly, birds of paradise are best known for the elaborate plumage that males use to attract a female. They also have a unique dance that they use to lure females, and often tickle them with their colorful feathers.

Porcupines have a very short mating season. Females are only interested in mating for eight to twelve hours per year. When females are ready to mate, they leave urine markings so that males can find them. A male will travel long distances to compete for a female. Male porcupines perform the unusual ritual of urinating on the female from a tree branch. If she is not interested in the male, she will scream and shake off the urine. If she is interested, the two will mate.

Seahorses are also unusual animals because it is the male that carries the eggs. Members of this species go through an elaborate courtship that lasts for days. When male and female seahorses are interested in each other, they hold tails, swim with their snouts together, and eventually change color to signal that they are ready to mate.

Evolution has not made mating a straightforward process. Though many single people complain about being alone, they can take comfort in the fact that they are not forced to endure the strange courting rituals that some animals must go through.

Reading Time: _______ minutes _______ seconds 339 words

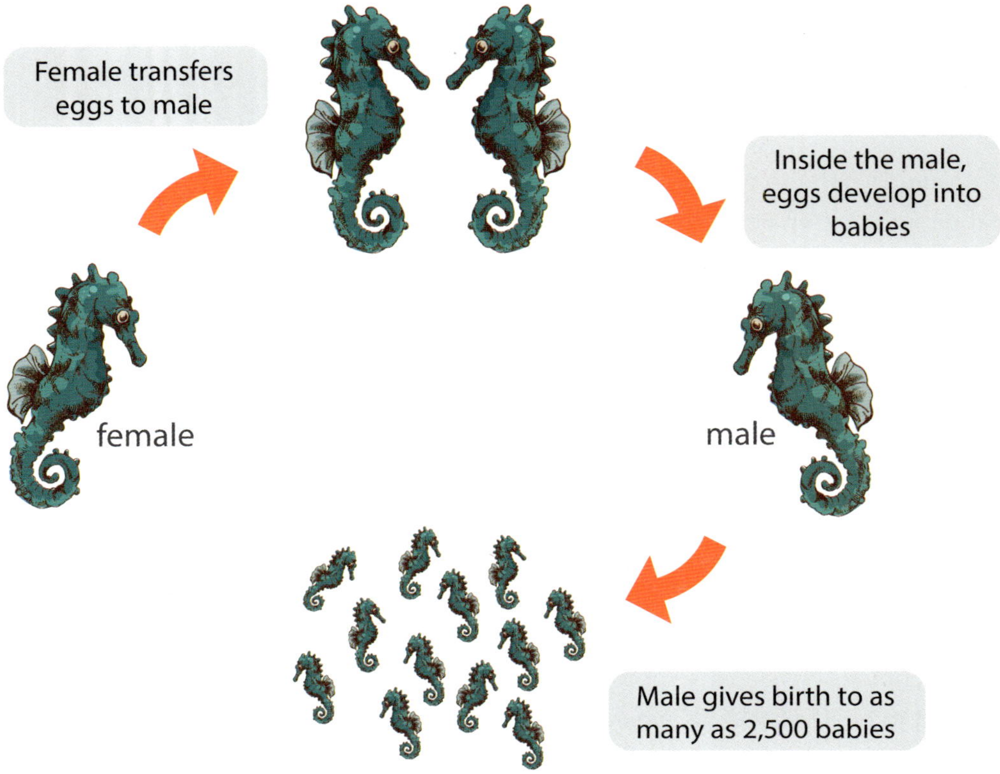

▲ The seahorse's mating process

Review the Highlights

◆ **Mark up the text and infographic according to the instructions.**

1. Look at Paragraph 1. Circle why animals need to mate.
2. Look at Paragraph 2. Circle the name of the animal that is romantic.
3. Look at Paragraph 2. Underline what birds of paradise do to lure a mate.
4. Look at Paragraph 3. Underline how long the mating season is for porcupines.
5. Look at Paragraph 4. Put a star next to who carries the eggs for seahorses after mating.
6. Look at the infographic. Write the maximum number of babies that a male seahorse might have at one time. ____________________

READING COMPREHENSION

A **Circle the correct answer.**

1. What is the main topic of the reading? Main idea
   a. Different courting rituals in the animal kingdom
   b. Birds that attract partners with their colorful feathers
   c. Straightforward mating processes
   d. Animals that use deception in order to find a mate

2. What do bowerbirds do to lure a mate? Details: what
   a. They travel a long way.
   b. They carry eggs.
   c. They build bowers.
   d. They urinate.

3. What do female porcupines do when they are ready to mate? Details: what
   a. They scream and shake.
   b. They change color.
   c. They leave urine markings.
   d. They urinate on the male from a tree branch.

4. Which of the following statements about courting rituals is NOT true? Negative fact
   a. Some animals are attracted to mates with colorful feathers.
   b. It is easy for animals to find a mate.
   c. Some animals use tactics or tricks to find a mate.
   d. There are animals that dance to attract a partner.

5. How do seahorses show their interest in each other? Details: how
   a. They carry each other's eggs.
   b. They hold tails and swim with their snouts together.
   c. The female changes into the same color as the male.
   d. The male swims in an elaborate pattern.

B **Complete the summary. Write the words from the reading that best fit in the blanks. One word is extra.**

romantic lure mate rituals offspring endure resort screams

Animals 1. ___________ to produce 2. ___________, but some animals must 3. ___________ to tricks or tactics to attract a mate. Some males perform elaborate 4. ___________ to attract females, while others have a unique appearance. For example, birds of paradise 5. ___________ females with their beautiful feathers. Sometimes they tickle them, too. Another strange courting ritual is that of the porcupine. Females leave urine markings when they are ready to mate. After a male responds, the female 6. ___________ if she is not interested in him. Luckily, people do not have to 7. ___________ the same courting rituals that some animals do.

SUMMARY

1. Discuss the following scenarios with a partner.

1. The best date you have ever been on or your ideal date
2. The worst date you have ever been on or the worst date you can imagine

2. Read the following introductory paragraph to a passage comparing human courting rituals to those of animals.

> What do you look for in a romantic partner? When you're on a first date, do you find yourself wondering how well the other person sings or dives? Dating and mating are very different in the animal kingdom than they are for humans. Animals and insects sometimes have very strange ways of finding mates. Male koalas attract females by singing to them in a deep voice. Great white sharks show off their diving skills for potential mates. Once an animal finds a mate, things can get even weirder. Male wasps hit their mates on the head. When bedbugs mate, the male stabs the female in the stomach violently.
>
> **Here is the first sentence of the next paragraph:**
>
> Dating for humans may not be so elaborate or violent, but it is just as strange.

3. With your partner, discuss what information you think will be included in this paragraph. What is strange about human dating rituals?

4. Using some of the points you discussed with your partner, complete the paragraph.

Dating for humans may not be so elaborate or violent, but it is just as strange.

____

____

____

____

VOCABULARY PRACTICE

Fill in the blanks with the words in the box. Change the form if necessary.

attract	courtship	unique	produce	per

1. Animals mate to ______________ offspring.
2. Some animals stand out because they look ______________.
3. The male bowerbirds will also dance for the female in an attempt to ______________ her.
4. Female porcupines are only interested in mating for eight to twelve hours ______________ year.
5. Members of this species go through an elaborate ______________ that lasts for days.

SPEAKING

3A Blind Date

A Authentic Text: Online advice column

Read the online advice column. Then discuss the advice with a partner. Do you have any other advice for Stressed Out?

Ask Ms. Trudy

Dear Ms. Trudy,

I'm going on a blind date this Friday night. We're going to have a typical dinner-and-movie date, and maybe we'll go to a café. The guy is my best friend's coworker, and she says he's perfect for me. We're both from Australia, and we are studying in the US right now. Also, we have the same major, business, and the same hobby, photography. But it's my first blind date. I'm a little shy with new people. Maybe I won't like him, or he won't like me. I can't stop worrying about it. I might cancel. What's your advice? Help!

- Stressed Out

Dear Stressed Out,

You shouldn't cancel the date. You're right—you may not like him very much, or he may not like you. But that's all right. Try to get to know each other. That will only happen if you relax and be yourself. If you're really nervous, you could ask your friend and her boyfriend to join you on a double date. Perhaps you'll feel more relaxed in a group.

Remember, it's only one evening. So have fun. If it doesn't go well, it's no big deal. And maybe you'll be less nervous on your next blind date.

- Ms. Trudy

speedy · 3 hours ago

0 0

Brief note

"It's no big deal" means it's not important (so don't worry about it).

B Vocabulary

Write the letters of the words and phrases from the box next to the correct definitions.

a. be yourself	b. get to know (someone)	c. cancel	d. double date	e. hobby
f. be stressed out	g. go on a blind date	h. shy	i. worry	j. perfect

1. to learn about a person and become friendly with each other ____
2. to go out with someone you don't know ____
3. to feel afraid that something bad may happen ____
4. to feel a lot of stress ____
5. something you like to do in your free time; a special interest ____
6. to decide not to go to a planned event ____
7. exactly right; having no bad points ____
8. to relax and not worry what others think ____
9. feeling nervous talking to others ____
10. a date that two couples go on together ____

C In Your World

Make a list of three things you would like to do on a blind date and three things you would not like to do. Then compare your ideas with a partner and discuss your reasons.

Me	
I'd like to	**I wouldn't like to**
______________________	______________________
______________________	______________________
______________________	______________________

Brief note

Sentence adverbs usually come at the beginning of a sentence or as part of a phrase at the end.

D Grammar

Making predictions and expressing probability with *will* and *be going to*

making predictions			
You can make a prediction (give an opinion about the future) using either *will* or *be going to*. *It'**ll rain** tomorrow.* *It'**s going to** rain tomorrow.*			
expressing probability			
maybe	**possibly**	**perhaps**	**probably**
Maybe is often used as a sentence adverb. It means that something is possible but not certain.	*Possibly* can be used after *will* or *be* verbs and as a sentence adverb. It's not used often in speaking.	*Perhaps* is like *maybe*, but it is used more often in writing than in conversation.	*Probably* is stronger than *maybe*, *possibly*, or *perhaps*. It means you are almost sure.
Maybe they are going to see a movie. I will talk to Jim or **maybe** his sister.	He will **possibly** call us tomorrow. He will call us tomorrow, **possibly**.	**Perhaps** you are going to need more money. We will buy some books and **perhaps** a magazine.	She will **probably** get the job. I am **probably** going to stay home on Sunday.

Brief note

One reason *will possibly* is not often spoken is because *might* or *may* is a more common way to say the same thing.

E Grammar Practice

Fill in the blanks with the words from the box. If more than one answer is possible, select the one that seems best.

possibly	will	is	maybe	probably

1. I think the guests ________________ have a good time.
2. Do you think he ________________ going to call you?
3. ________________ she will enjoy dinner at an Indian restaurant.
4. She's sick, so she's ________________ going to cancel the dinner party.
5. We are ________________ going to get a German car, or perhaps an Italian one. We're not sure.

F Use the Language

Going on a date

Read the following dating situations. What advice do you have for these people? What will probably happen if they take your advice? What if they don't? Make notes about your advice and predictions on a separate piece of paper.

Emma: For our second date, a guy invited me to an art museum. He knows a lot about art, but I don't. What should I do?

Fred: I went on a blind date at my favorite restaurant. She was very interesting, but she was not nice to our waiter. Should I go out with her again?

Pedro: A girl invited me on a bike ride. I really like her—but I can't ride a bike. I'm worried about telling her. Any advice?

Now compare your ideas with a partner's. Report your ideas to the class.

WRITING

Below are some facts pertaining to Korean coffee habits. After reading through them, answer the questions to complete two paragraphs stating your own coffee habits. Use the questions as a guide, and add details wherever appropriate. Be prepared to read your paragraphs to class.

Things to Think About

- Koreans generally prefer milder coffee than Americans do.
- Coffee houses in Korea are open late, and many until midnight.
- Coffee houses are busy morning to night with office workers and young people.
- During the frigid Korean winter, Koreans order cappuccinos, café lattes, teas, and café mochas. In the hot summers, they enjoy iced coffee and ice-blended drinks.
- Many coffee houses now offer high-speed wireless Internet service.
- Coffee house décor often resembles a living room, which creates a comfortable atmosphere.

What is your favorite caffeinated beverage?
Why is it your favorite?
How do you like it? Strong? With sugar?
When do you usually have this beverage?
Do your preferences change in winter or summer? How?
Where do you normally get these beverages? Why?
What do you do while you are drinking your beverage?
What are some things you like about coffee shops?
What are some things you don't like about coffee shops?

SUPPLEMENTAL READING

Keimyung University's Principles of Living Standards

Track 13

Cleanliness

Cleanliness means 'being clean and pure,' referring to a state free from impurities. Particularly as the world transforms into a 'global village' with fewer barriers between nations, public health and safety is becoming a growing concern.

Integrity

Integrity means 'being upright and straightforward without deceit or falsehood.' It is considered a very precious value in life across Eastern and Western cultures. As the saying goes, 'Integrity is indeed the best policy,' the importance of honesty is increasing in the lives of modern individuals.

Frugality

Frugality means 'not wasting resources and using them only when necessary.' We live in an era where the abuse of energy, materials, and goods is depleting our natural resources. Therefore, frugality has become one of the most important virtues in our lives.

Harmony

Harmony refers to 'the merging of different kinds into one without distinction.' In recent years, the term 'harmony' has been widely used across various fields and sectors to promote interdisciplinary research, improve organizational productivity, and achieve mutual goals.

EXTENSION Talk or Write About It

1. Which of the four principles of living standards do you think is most important in your life? Why?
2. How can Keimyung students show honesty and integrity in their daily lives on campus? Can you give some examples?
3. What principle would you add to the list? Why?

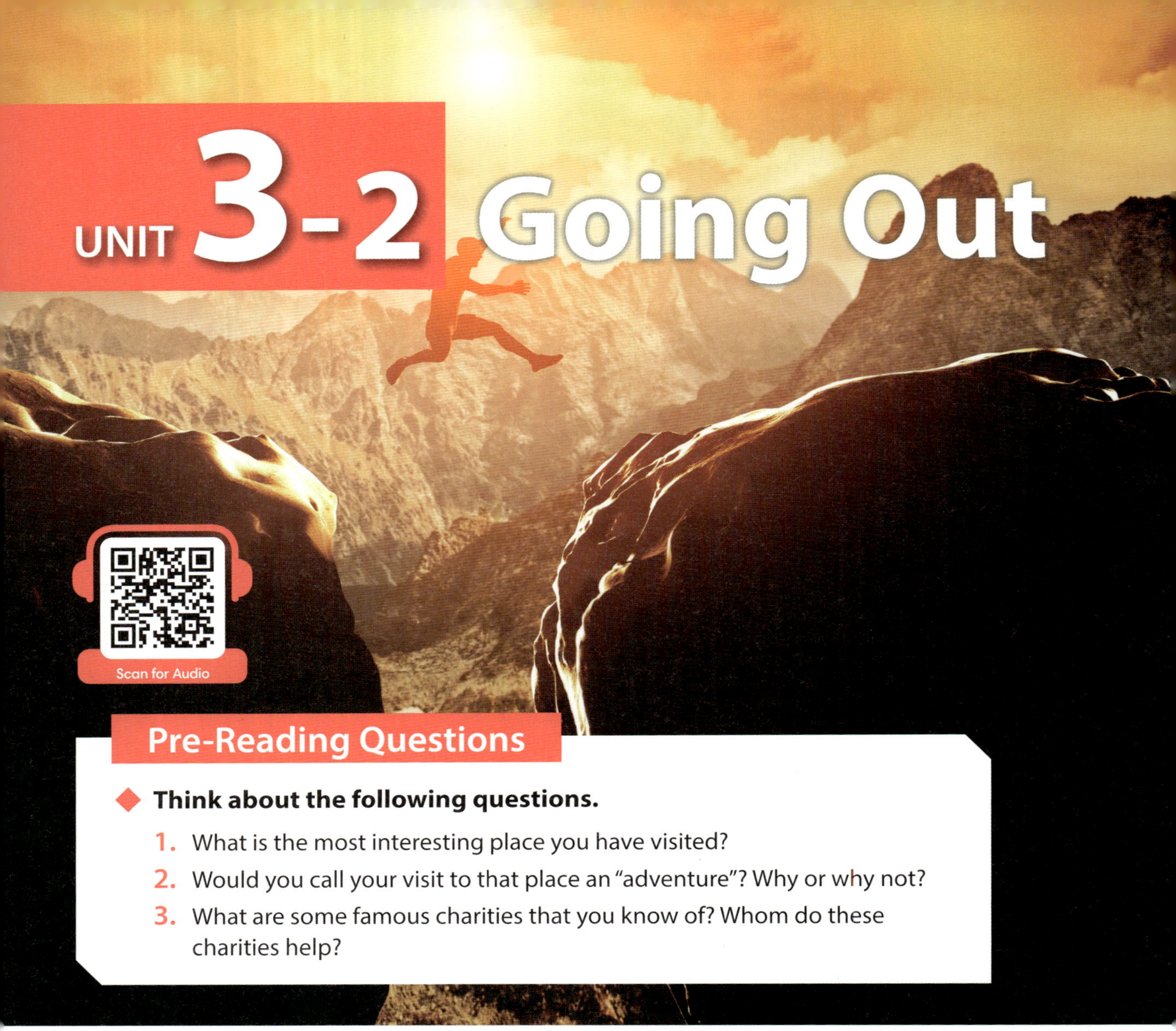

UNIT 3-2 Going Out

Scan for Audio

Pre-Reading Questions

◆ **Think about the following questions.**

1. What is the most interesting place you have visited?
2. Would you call your visit to that place an "adventure"? Why or why not?
3. What are some famous charities that you know of? Whom do these charities help?

VOCABULARY PREVIEW

◆ **Match each word with the correct definition.**

1. capitalism •	• a. used to describe something (such as an agreement) that will happen only if something else happens
2. bargain •	• b. an economic system in which land, factories, etc., are owned by individuals and companies rather than by the government
3. conditional •	• c. the degree to which something is right and good
4. entrant •	• d. an arrangement in which a person or organization agrees to give money to someone for participating in a charity event
5. morality •	• e. something bought for a good price; an advantageous purchase
6. sponsorship •	• f. a person who enters a competition

ADVENTURE TOURS FOR CHARITY

Track 14

In almost any magazine or newspaper in England, you can find advertisements for adventure tours to **exotic**[1] places. These exciting tours can be bicycling, hiking, or even motorcycle trips across deserts, over mountains, and around live volcanoes! Many of these tours are **conditional** on a requirement that makes them more interesting to some people—you must raise money for **charity**[2] first.

One advertisement offers people something called the "Scottish Highlands Triple Challenge." The advertisement describes it as a weekend of cycling, **trekking**[3], and canoeing, ending at the top of Ben Nevis, the highest mountain in the UK. The organization that sets up this tour is advertising for people who can give time and effort to raising money for a good cause. For their hard work, these people will also be able to take the holiday of a lifetime.

The first thing that people have to do is sign up for the tour. The number of people who can go on each tour is limited, and many tours fill up fast. Those who sign up then have to pay a **deposit**[4] of £350 (US$480) in order to hold their place on the tour. People cannot get their deposit back later if they change their minds, so

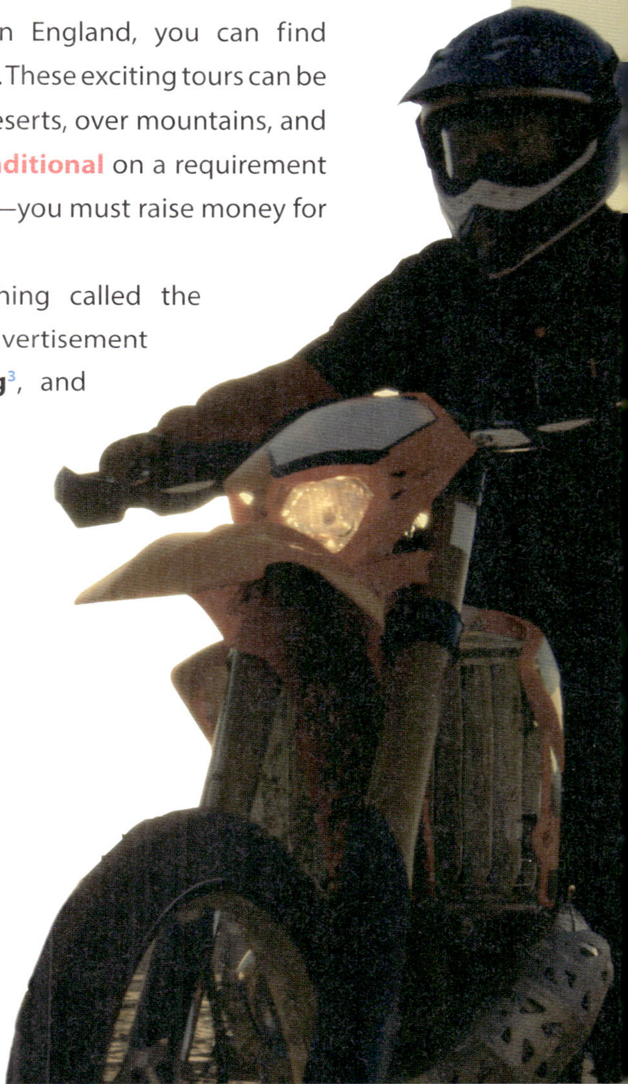

1	**exotic**	*adj.*	very different, strange, or unusual
2	**charity**	*n.*	the act of giving money, food, or other help to people who are poor, sick, etc.; an organization that helps others
3	**trek**	*v.*	to travel by walking for pleasure and adventure
4	**deposit**	*n.*	money given as a promise or a down payment for something

they had better be sure they really want to go.

Next, each person must choose a charity and raise a minimum amount of money for it. They can choose from a long list of organizations working on important causes, from animal shelters to medical care for the **elderly**[5]. The required amount is usually between £1,500 and £2,500 (US$2,000 to $3,500). In order to raise this much money, some people send letters to friends and relatives asking for **sponsorships**. Other people have big parties where all of the guests must pay **admission**[6]—or they even hold contests. One farmer divided up his field into one-meter squares to raise money. People could buy one square of the field for £1 each. Then the farmer let his cow walk across the field. The **entrant** who had bought the square where the cow dropped its first "cow patty" won a prize. Surprisingly, the majority of people who go on the adventure tours end up collecting more than the minimum money required.

Q Underline two examples of causes that people can raise money for.

Some people question the **morality** of this system, saying that it is wrong for part of the money that people collect to be used for someone's vacation. However, the companies try to keep the overall cost of the tours low so that at least sixty or seventy percent of the money that is raised goes to the charity. Why not mix **capitalism** with giving, they ask? One company, which runs ten to fifteen tours a year, said they make about £50,000 on each one.

Q How much of the money raised is given to the charity?

Do people really want to spend their vacations doing something like bicycling for 400 kilometers when they could be **lounging**[7] on a beach? These tours are not for everybody. But the people who sign up for them all agree that it is a great experience.

After trekking across the Namib Desert, a young construction worker from London cried as he hugged all of the other people in his tour group. Everyone cried. Most of them never thought that they could take part in an adventure like that. They had not only completed a once-in-a-lifetime trip, but the price they paid for it was to help someone in need. To them, that's a great **bargain**.

Reading Time: _______ minutes _______ seconds   573 words

[5] **elderly** *n.* older people
[6] **admission** *n.* the cost of entering a theater, event, etc.
[7] **lounge** *v.* to sit or lie in a relaxed way

READING COMPREHENSION

A **Mark each statement as true (T) or false (F) according to the reading.**

1. _____ The charities set no limit on the number of people who can go on each tour, so some tours get very crowded.
2. _____ People who want to go on an adventure tour for charity must pay a deposit first.
3. _____ The farmer described in the reading sold his cow to raise money for the charity.
4. _____ Most people fail to raise the minimum amount of money for the charity.
5. _____ Less than half of the money that people raise for the charity is used to pay for expenses on the trip.

B **Choose the best answer according to the reading.**

1. What is the main purpose of the reading? PURPOSE
   a. To compare tours arranged by two charities
   b. To describe a dangerous tour set up by a charity
   c. To explain how charities raise money through tours
   d. To give information about interesting places to visit

2. Which is NOT true about charity adventure tours? DETAIL
   a. They make more money for companies than charities.
   b. They involve activities such as biking and canoeing.
   c. They benefit a variety of different charities.
   d. They are fairly cheap for the companies to run.

3. Which is NOT mentioned as a way to raise the charity money? DETAIL
   a. Having parties at which the guests have to pay
   b. Asking for money from your loved ones
   c. Holding some kind of contest
   d. Selling things you don't need anymore

4. We can guess that these trips are "not for everybody" because _______. INFERENCE
   a. they are very expensive
   b. they involve traveling with a group
   c. they are difficult rather than relaxing
   d. they are for charities that not everyone likes

C **Look for the answers in the reading and write them on the lines.**

1. Why should people be careful when they pay a deposit for a charity adventure tour?

   ____

2. Why do some people disagree with this method of raising money for charities?

   ____

SUMMARY

An introductory sentence for a brief summary of the passage is given below. Choose three more sentences to complete the summary.

First Sentence: Many travel tours in England offer adventures to people who agree to raise money for charity.

1. People interested in a tour must pay a deposit that is returned if they decide not to go on the trip.
2. People choose a charity and raise a minimum amount by holding events or asking for sponsorships.
3. Charities usually require travelers to raise a minimum of $4,000 before they can go on the trip.
4. Although the trips are usually not easy, travelers love the experience and the feeling of helping others.
5. Some critics don't like this way of raising money, but the companies say most of the money raised goes to charity.

VOCABULARY PRACTICE

Fill in the blanks with the words in the box. Change the form if necessary.

morality	conditional	entrant	sponsorship	bargain	capitalism

1. Janet has a(n) ________________ agreement with her parents that she will get $20 a week if she does her chores.
2. Some people support making gambling legal even if they question its ________________.
3. At forty percent off the original price, this beautiful winter coat is a real ________________.
4. Each ________________ in the art contest must submit his or her work by the October 1 deadline.
5. I managed to get three ________________ for the charity marathon, which will bring in hundreds of dollars.
6. Since the fall of the Soviet Union in 1991, Russia has made the difficult change from communism to ________________.

SPEAKING

3B Visiting Relatives

A Model Conversation

Read the conversation. Then listen. Track 15

Brief note

"Thanksgiving" is a US holiday in late November. Families get together to eat a big meal, usually including turkey.

Craig: Hi, Sandra. Happy Thanksgiving.

Sandra: You, too! Are you and Marie on your way?

Craig: No, Marie and the kids are still getting ready. I'm calling to say we'll be a little late.

Sandra: That's okay. Actually, I still have a lot of work to do for dinner. I'm running late, too, because I'm chatting online with my grandchildren in California.

Craig: Oh, how are they? And their parents? I miss them.

Sandra: Fantastic. The kids are going to visit next month for a week, so we can look forward to that.

Craig: Great! Nina and John are my only niece and nephew, but I hardly ever see them. Hey, maybe I'll take them to a football game.

Sandra: Yes, they'll love that. So, anyway, what time will you get here?

Craig: We'll be there at about 4:30. Want us to bring anything?

Sandra: No, that's all right. Just be ready to eat a lot.

Craig: We're looking forward to the turkey. I always tell everyone about my mother-in-law's great cooking.

Brief note

A person's "mother-in-law" is the mother of his or her spouse. The word *in-law* can be used with other family words, too. For example, your spouse's brother or your sibling's husband is your *brother-in-law*.

B Vocabulary

Look at the family tree. Then fill in the blanks with the correct words from the box.

niece	mother-in-law	nephew	grandchildren (*sing.* grandchild)

1. Sandra is Craig's ________________.
2. Sandra and her husband have four ________________.
3. Nina is Craig and Marie's ________________.
4. Craig and Marie have a ________________ named John.

Match the words and phrases with the correct definitions.

5. be on (one's) way •
6. look forward to (something) •
7. run late •
8. miss •

• **a.** to think about (a future event) in a happy way
• **b.** to feel sad because someone isn't with you
• **c.** to be late getting ready; to be behind schedule
• **d.** to be going or traveling somewhere

C About You

Tell a partner about your relatives.

1. Do you have any brothers-in-law or sisters-in-law? What are they like?
2. How many nieces and nephews do your parents have? How many grandchildren? Do they visit your parents often?
3. What do you do when you visit your relatives?

D Grammar

Future tense

<table>
<tr><th colspan="2">future tense with will and be going to</th></tr>
<tr><td colspan="2">We can speak about the future using will or be going to. Often, you can use either will or be going to:
We'll be a little late. We're going to be a little late.</td></tr>
<tr><th>will</th><th>be going to</th></tr>
<tr><td>With if (first conditional):
If you're late again, mom will be upset.</td><td rowspan="2">For decisions and definite plans made before speaking:
I've packed my suitcase. I'm going to leave soon.
Often, the present continuous has the same meaning:
I've packed my suitcase. I'm leaving soon.</td></tr>
<tr><td>For offers to do something:
Those bags look heavy. I'll help you.</td></tr>
</table>

E Grammar Practice

Circle the correct answers.

1. (We're going to / We'll) sell our car. We put an ad in the newspaper.
2. I think maybe (I'm going to / I'll) cook Thanksgiving dinner this year.
3. If you don't study now, you (aren't / won't be) ready for the final exam.
4. They've put on their shoes. They (are going to / will) head out.
5. A: I'm running late for class, and I still have to take the dog for a walk.
   B: No, go to class. (I'll / I'm going to) take him.

F Read to Write

1. **Read the email about a family get-together. Underline the future tense verbs.**

> Hey, Lucas.
>
> Thanks for inviting me to visit this weekend, but I won't be able to come. Saturday is my sister's 25th birthday, and we're going to give her a big party. It was my future brother-in-law's idea. He and my sister are going to get married in June. On Saturday, we're going to have dinner at her favorite restaurant and then go to her apartment to have cake and hang out. (I'm going to make the cake!) Maybe we'll play some games. It'll be fun. My aunts, uncles, nieces, and nephews will be there. I'm looking forward to it because I don't see them very often. Anyway, let's get together soon. I'll call you.
>
> Alicia

2. **Now look at the pictures below. What kind of family get-together would you like to have this weekend? Choose one. Who will come? What will you do? On a separate sheet of paper, write an email to a friend like the one above.**

A barbecue at home

A hiking and/or camping trip

A day at the beach

MEMO

WRITING

1. What are good activities for a first date?

2. What are good places for dates?

SUPPLEMENTAL READING

Help Yourself by Helping Others

Track 16

Most of us are taught that we should be giving and helpful to others because it is the right thing to do. But it turns out that by helping other people, we benefit ourselves in multiple ways as well.

Behaving in a kind and generous way simply makes people feel good. In a 2008 experiment at Harvard Business School, participants who gave money to someone else ended up in a better mood than those who spent it on themselves. This was no surprise to the happiness expert Dr. Sonja Lyubormirsky. She advocates doing acts of kindness as one of the most reliable ways of becoming happier—and of building connections with others, which increases happiness even more. In 2012, Lyubormirsky published a study on nine-to-eleven-year-old children. After doing acts of kindness for several weeks, they were not only happier but also more popular.

Giving your time to charity can even make you physically healthier. Research has found that helping someone can actually decrease stress and lower blood pressure. This effect may be especially important for older people. A study on elderly couples found that those who did volunteer work were much less likely to die over a five-year period than those who didn't, and this was true regardless of age, exercise habits, and general health. Interestingly, the study found no link between receiving help and living longer. Apparently, as the saying goes, it really is better to give than to receive.

Fill in the blanks with information from the reading.

1. Being kind to others makes people ______________________.
2. Children in one study were both ______________________ and ______________________ after doing acts of kindness for a few weeks.
3. In another study, older people who did ______________________ lived longer.

EXTENSION Talk or Write About It

Have you ever helped a charity? How? Do you have any goals that involve helping others? What are they?

UNIT 4-1 Health and Medicine

Scan for Audio

Pre-Reading Questions

◆ **Think about the following questions.**

1. What are some health problems caused by too much body fat?
2. How can you tell if someone's weight is unhealthy?
3. What do you think BMI is?

VOCABULARY PREVIEW

◆ **Match each word with the correct definition.**

1. diagnose	a. to put information (such as a word or a number) into something
2. gauge	b. a small electronic device used for adding, subtracting, etc.
3. thickness	c. simple and basic in a way that is true but not complete
4. crude	d. to identify a disease or other health condition in someone
5. calculator	e. a measurement of how thick something is
6. plug into	f. to measure or judge

BODY MASS AND WEIGHT

Track 17

To be obese means to have too much fat on the body. Obese people are not just overweight—they are so overweight that they are likely to develop health problems. The **precise**[1] cause of the recent rise in obesity is not clear, but it is certain that obesity is a problem in most countries. A recent study **estimated**[2] that about forty-two percent of people in the US are obese. People need to understand what obesity is and how to tell if they themselves are obese so that they can change their condition.

An obese person does not always look extremely fat. Even people who seem only slightly overweight can be **diagnosed** as obese. If you have a certain percentage of fat on your body, then your health might be in danger. This is usually thought to be about forty percent of the body's total **composition**[3].

Most people still rely on just their weight measurement to tell if they are overweight or obese, but there are problems with this **method**[4]. There are different recommended weights for different ages, and weight alone says nothing about a person's percentage of body fat, which is most important. Directly figuring out body fat percentage can be quite difficult. For example, one method requires you to **squeeze**[5] the fat on the back of your arm, measure its **thickness**, and then **plug** this number **into** a **formula**[6]. However, this is only a **crude** estimate; a truly accurate measurement of body fat percentage requires an X-ray.

Q Underline two ways of measuring body fat.

Q How is a person's BMI determined?

1	**precise**	*adj.*	very accurate and exact
2	**estimate**	*v.*	to guess
3	**composition**	*n.*	the combination of parts or elements that make up something
4	**method**	*n.*	a way of doing something
5	**squeeze**	*v.*	to press together the parts and especially the opposite sides of something
6	**formula**	*n.*	in math, a general fact or rule expressed in letters and numbers

Another popular method of **gauging** whether someone is obese is the Body Mass Index (BMI). BMI is a person's weight in kilograms divided by the square of his or her height in meters. A normal BMI for a healthy adult is generally between twenty and twenty-five. A BMI of thirty or more means a person is obese. Many experts feel that BMI is a reliable way to determine if a person's weight is unhealthy, while others feel that BMI is too general to be really useful. The numbers come from comparisons of large groups of people. BMI is not related to an individual's body composition, so it says nothing about a person's actual percentage of body fat.

People have different body types, which can make BMI unreliable. For instance, athletes usually have more muscle mass than other people, and muscle weighs more than fat. Therefore, an athlete may have a high BMI, but this does not mean they are not healthy. Some people have higher bone **density**[7] than others, which also increases their weight. In some cases, those who have very low body fat and are also not muscular can have a BMI that is too high. BMI is also unreliable for children and the elderly, so even supporters of BMI think that it should not be used for people under eighteen or over seventy years old.

Despite these criticisms, there are strong positive aspects of BMI. The main one is that it is very simple. The formula can be used easily and does not take special knowledge or equipment—just a scale, along with a pencil and paper or a **calculator**. Though BMI is a general measurement, it still gives useful information and can help identify when there might be a problem. Furthermore, some studies have shown that people with higher BMI numbers have a higher risk of health problems. It takes only a minute to get a BMI number, but the results can be very important to a person's life.

What is this paragraph mainly about?

a. Which people can benefit from measuring their BMI

b. Why BMI is useful even though it isn't perfect

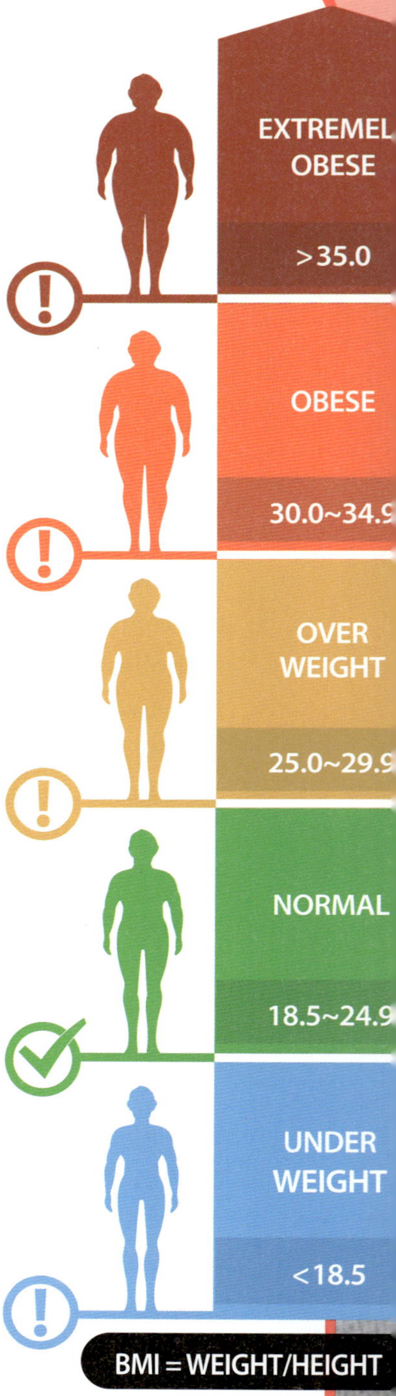

Reading Time: _______ minutes _______ seconds 580 words

[7] **density** *n.* the amount of matter in something that is shown by the relationship between its weight and its size

READING COMPREHENSION

A **Mark each statement as true (T) or false (F) according to the reading.**

1. ______ More than half of Americans are obese.
2. ______ It is easy to tell whether someone is obese by looking at them.
3. ______ Obesity can be defined as having at least forty percent body fat.
4. ______ The most precise way to measure body fat is by the thickness of arm fat.
5. ______ An X-ray is necessary in order to measure BMI.

B **Choose the best answer according to the reading.**

1. What is the main purpose of the reading? PURPOSE
   a. To discuss different methods for dieting and losing weight
   b. To give examples of health problems caused by eating too much
   c. To describe the squeezing method for measuring fat percentage
   d. To explain why BMI is generally a useful method for measuring obesity

2. In paragraph 4, the word *it* refers to ______. REFERENCE
   a. BMI
   b. individual
   c. body composition
   d. comparison

3. Which group of people may have a high BMI but still be healthy? DETAIL
   a. Obese people
   b. Very muscular people
   c. People with low bone density
   d. Most young adults

4. What is an advantage of BMI over other measurement methods? DETAIL
   a. It is based on the individual's body.
   b. It measures both muscle and fat.
   c. It does not require special equipment or skills.
   d. It works for all ages and body types.

C **Look for the answers in the reading and write them on the lines.**

1. What is the normal BMI range for an adult?

   ____

2. For whom do supporters of BMI think that it should NOT be used?

   ____

SUMMARY

An introductory sentence for a brief summary of the passage is given below. Choose three more sentences to complete the summary.

First Sentence: There are different methods of determining whether a person is obese.

1. A muscular person weighs more because muscles are much denser than fat.
2. Most people still rely only on a person's weight as a method for determining obesity, although it is considered inaccurate.
3. The Body Mass Index (BMI) compares a person's weight with his or her height, and the resulting number is compared with that of an average person.
4. According to a study, about forty-two percent of Americans are considered to be obese.
5. Although it is not precise, the BMI still gives a person useful information about his or her body.

VOCABULARY PRACTICE

Fill in the blanks with the words in the box. Change the form if necessary.

calculator	crude	diagnose	gauge	plug into	thickness

1. I've made a ____________ outline of my essay but haven't figured out the details yet.
2. This time only, students will be allowed to use their ____________ during the math quiz.
3. When the number 3 is ____________ the expression $4x^2 - 2x$, the result is 30.
4. Thanks to the ____________ of the walls in this building, we can't hear our neighbors, and they can't hear us.
5. It's hard to ____________ how heavy a sofa is just by looking at it.
6. Millions of people are ____________ with skin cancer every year, but most survive.

SPEAKING

4A Making a Doctor's Appointment

A Model Conversation

Read the conversation. Then listen. Track 18

Receptionist: Dr. Jackson's office. How can I help you?
Patient: Hello. I'd like to make an appointment to see the doctor.
Receptionist: Have you been here before?
Patient: Yes, I have.
Receptionist: Okay. What's your name and date of birth?
Patient: Samuel Chapman, May 13th, 1990.
Receptionist: And what's the reason for your visit?
Patient: I've had a nasty headache since last week. I'm not sure what to do. I've tried different medications, but they haven't helped.
Receptionist: Sounds like the flu. Do you have any other symptoms—vomiting or trouble breathing?
Patient: No, just the pain.
Receptionist: Have you ever experienced a similar headache before?
Patient: No. I'm usually very healthy. Could I see the doctor today?
Receptionist: Yes, we've just had a cancellation. Can you come at 3:00?

Brief note
A "symptom" is any feeling or change in the body that happens when you are sick.

B Vocabulary

Look at the pictures and listen to the words. Then write the correct word under each picture. Track 19

patient illness headache medication/medicine vomit

____

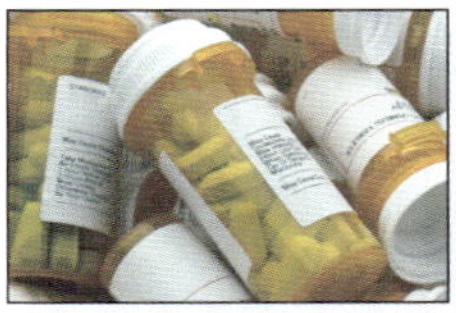
____

____

____

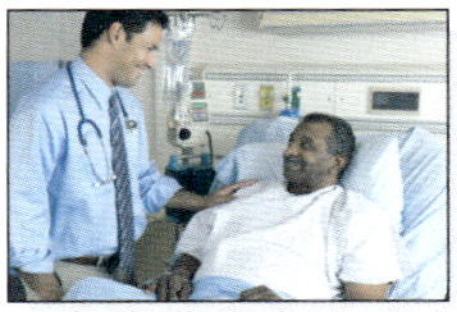
____

Match the words with the correct definitions.

1. trouble breathing •	• **a.** the act of stopping something that has been planned
2. nasty •	• **b.** alike; seeming the same or almost the same
3. flu •	• **c.** being unable to breathe (take air into the body) easily
4. cancellation •	• **d.** very bad; very serious or painful
5. similar •	• **e.** an illness like a cold, but more serious

C Comprehension

Read the statements about the conversation and circle true or false. Check your answers with a partner.

1. Samuel is Dr. Jackson's patient. true false
2. He hasn't taken any medicine yet. true false
3. He has several symptoms. true false
4. He will be able to see the doctor this afternoon. true false

D Grammar

Brief note

For regular verbs, the past participle is the same as the simple past form. Some verbs are irregular.

Present perfect tense

present perfect		
You use the present perfect tense to talk about past events that have a connection to the present. The form of the present perfect is *have/has* + past participle.		
meaning	**common expressions**	**examples**
past state/action that continues to the present	*for* + period of time *since* + point in time	She **has worked** here for three years. I**'ve had** a terrible headache since last week.
experience	*before, ever, never, once, twice, ~ times*	A: **Have** you (ever) **been** there before? B: Yes, I **have**. / No, I**'ve** never **been** there. I**'ve tried** medications, but they **haven't helped**.
change over time	*since* + point in time	The baby**'s grown** so much since last month!
completed actions	*already, yet*	I**'ve** already **finished** my project. **Have** you **started** yours yet?
recent events with an effect on the present; news	*just*	He**'s broken** his leg. We**'ve** just **had** a cancellation.

E Grammar Practice

Underline the errors and rewrite the sentences correctly using the present perfect tense.

1. I've feel sick since last night. ______________________
2. He has had a headache for this morning. ______________________
3. Have you went to the hospital? ______________________
4. Has you just booked an appointment with the doctor? ______________________
5. Jake has broke his leg. ______________________
6. She hasn't saw the doctor yet. ______________________

F Use the Language

Sick day

Tell a partner about the last time you were sick and what you did to feel better.

Take notes on your partner's story. Then write a short story summarizing your partner's sick day.

Notes: Partner's story	Short story

WRITING

You can choose one of the topics below. (Partners can choose the same topic, but they do not have to.) Questions have been provided. Record your partner's answers on the lines below. When you are done, your partner will interview you. When you are both done, share your answers with the class.

Partner: ____________________ **Topic:** ____________________

Topic A: Korea's Health Care Needs Help!

1. What causes the problem of overcrowding in Korean clinics and hospitals? Give examples. How do you think this problem can be solved?

   ____

   ____

2. Why do people take too much medication that they may not need? List at least two reasons. How can this be prevented?

   ____

   ____

3. What is hypochondria, and why are there so many cases in Korea? Why is it a problem for the health care system? How can we deal with it?

   ____

   ____

Topic B: Korea's Health Care is Wonderful!

1. Why do you think Korea's health care is so good? List specific reasons.

   ____

   ____

2. Korea has one of the best health care systems in Asia. How is this apparent? Explain.

   ____

   ____

3. If you were sick, why would you prefer to be treated in a Korean hospital instead of an American one? What advantages would you have?

   ____

   ____

SUPPLEMENTAL READING

Keimyung Medical Missionary Museum

Track 20

In the early 20th century, missionaries introduced Western medicine to Daegu along with Christianity. The houses where these missionaries lived and worked are now preserved on the hill of Dongsan Campus. The three red-brick tile-roofed houses each hold over 100 years of history. Since 1999, they have been designated as tangible cultural heritage sites by the city of Daegu, and they currently serve as museums.

Each of the three houses is organized as a themed museum. The Switzer House is a missionary museum, where missionary Switzer lived, along with the principal of Gyesung School and the dean of Keimyung University. The house exhibits photos related to the history of Protestantism, various types of Bibles, and missionary artifacts. The Blair House, where Reverend Blair lived, recreates a traditional Joseon Seodang (village school) and an elementary school classroom from the 1960s and 1970s. It also displays textbooks from different periods, folk materials, and photos from the March 1st Independence Movement in the Daegu area. The Chamness House, where Reverend Chamness and the director of Dongsan Hospital lived, houses a large collection of Eastern and Western medical instruments from around the 1900s. Due to its picturesque surroundings, this area has been used as a filming location for various movies and was selected as a 'Star of Korean Tourism' in 2012.

Source: 빛을 여는 계명인. 계명대학교 출판부. 2024. p.226–228.

EXTENSION Talk or Write About It

1. Which Daegu cultural heritage sites do you know about?
2. Do you like to visit museums? Which ones?
3. Have you seen any of the television programs or movies filmed on location at The Keimyung Medical Missionary Museum or Keimyung University?

UNIT 4-2 Health and Medicine

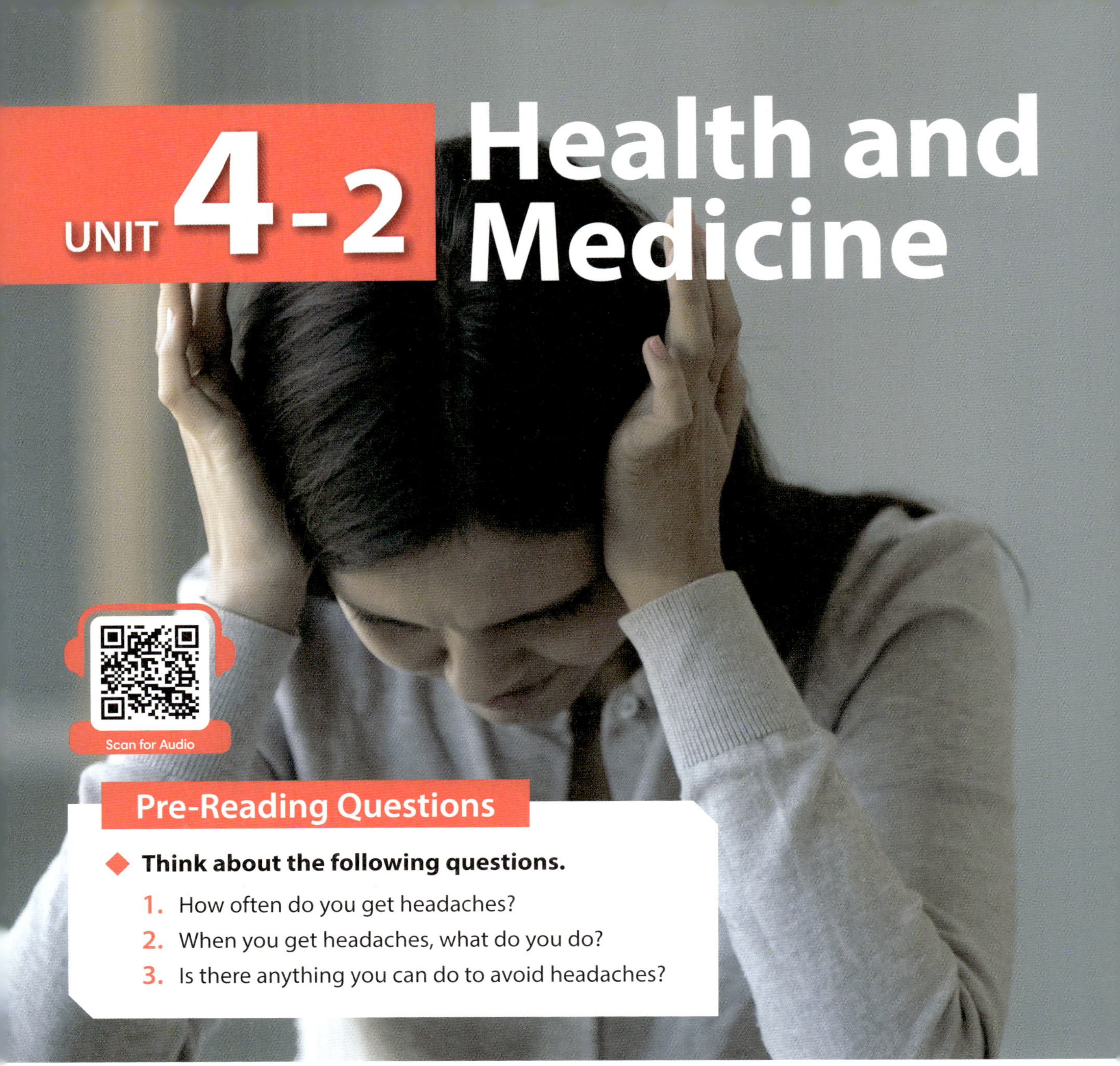

Scan for Audio

Pre-Reading Questions

◆ **Think about the following questions.**

1. How often do you get headaches?
2. When you get headaches, what do you do?
3. Is there anything you can do to avoid headaches?

VOCABULARY PREVIEW

◆ **Match each word with the correct definition.**

1. tumor	a. something that causes a change or a reaction
2. chemistry	b. a mass of tissue in or on the body that is made of abnormal cells
3. acid	c. a chemical with a sour taste that forms a salt when mixed with a base
4. physiological	d. the rate at which work is completed
5. productivity	e. the structure and properties of a substance
6. stimulus (*pl.* stimuli)	f. of or relating to how a living thing or its parts function

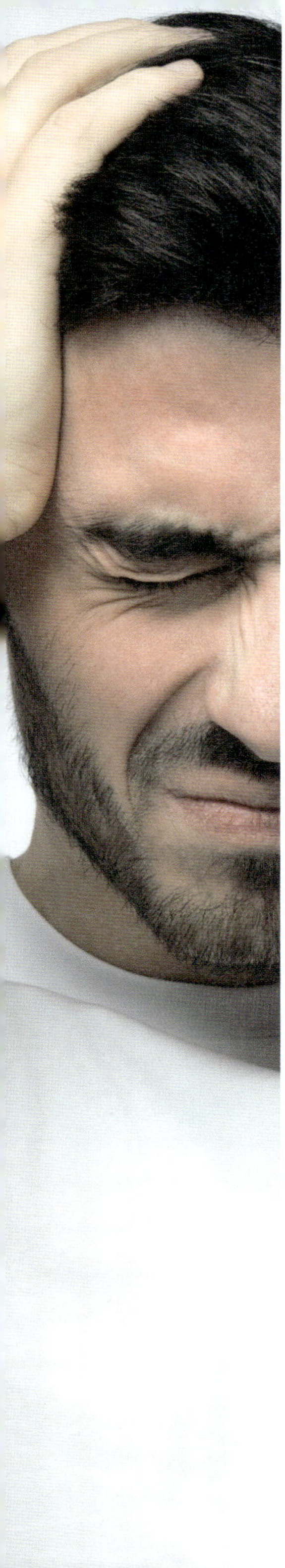

STUDYING HEADACHES

Track 21

Headaches are a big problem. Each year, millions of people suffer from **severe**[1] headaches that affect their enjoyment of life, not to mention their **productivity** at work. In fact, according to one estimate, headaches cost individuals and businesses more than $50 billion each year! This is one of the reasons research into headaches has become a worldwide effort.

Although he did not know much about how headaches work, **Hippocrates**[2] was the first doctor to find a way to treat them. By 400 BCE, Hippocrates had discovered that the **bark**[3] from **willow trees**[4] was useful in treating pain. He made a white powder from the tree's bark and gave it to his patients.

Q **What happened in the 1800s that helped headache sufferers?**

Hippocrates did not know it, but he was actually prescribing a natural chemical in willow bark called salicin. When a person eats salicin, the chemical is changed inside his or her body into salicylic **acid**. It turns out that salicylic acid is good for stopping pain, including headache pain, but it is bad for a person's stomach. In the 1800s, a chemist in Germany slightly changed the acid's form to make it easier for people to take. This new form of the chemical was called acetylsalicylic acid, now commonly known as **aspirin**[5].

Aspirin was used throughout most of the 1900s to treat headaches, but doctors had little idea about what really caused headaches. When doctors

1	**severe**	*adj.*	strong; very bad
2	**Hippocrates**	*n.*	a Greek doctor who started the study of medicine
3	**bark**	*n.*	the outer covering of a tree
4	**willow tree**	*n.*	a tree with long, narrow leaves and strong, thin branches
5	**aspirin**	*n.*	a medicine that reduces pain and fever

can diagnose the cause of a disease, they can find better ways to treat it. Therefore, as medical technology developed, doctors began to use it to learn more about the human brain and about headaches.

Underline two possible causes of a secondary headache.

Currently, doctors **classify**[6] headaches into two general types: primary and secondary. A primary headache is a condition suffered as only the headache itself. On the other hand, a secondary headache is one caused by another **physiological** condition, such as an infection or a **tumor**.

For primary headaches, doctors have determined three possible causes. One kind of primary headache is caused by stress. Doctors usually call these **tension**[7] headaches, and they are **characteristically**[8] felt on both sides of the head as a dull, steady pain.

Another kind of primary headache is the migraine headache. Exactly what causes these headaches is not well understood, but many experts believe it could be abnormal brain activity causing changes in the brain's **chemistry** and blood flow. For many people, migraines are **triggered**[9] by certain **stimuli**, such as poor sleep or particular foods or smells. A sufferer usually feels intense pain on one side of the head and becomes sensitive to light and noise. If the migraine is severe, the sufferer may **vomit**[10] repeatedly.

Who is more likely to be affected by cluster headaches?

The third kind of primary headache is known as the cluster headache. Cluster headaches typically occur around the same time each day for weeks or months at a time. The person suffering from this kind of headache usually feels pain on one side of her or his head, and the pain is centered around one of the eyes. Doctors do not know much at present about cluster headaches, but they seem to be more common among men and could be related to alcohol or other things that affect a person's blood flow.

Using computers and more advanced medical equipment, doctors continue to learn more about what happens in the brain before and during headaches. Especially in the case of migraines, some doctors believe they have found the part of the brain that sets off the reaction for severe attacks. With these insights into brain processes, doctors hope new ways will be discovered to stop headaches before they begin.

Reading Time: _______ minutes _______ seconds 588 words

6	**classify**	*v.*	to arrange into groups based on similarities
7	**tension**	*n.*	stress
8	**characteristically**	*adv.*	usually; typically
9	**trigger**	*v.*	to cause to begin
10	**vomit**	*v.*	to empty the contents of one's stomach through the mouth; to throw up

READING COMPREHENSION

A **Mark each statement as true (T) or false (F) according to the reading.**

1. _____ The first treatment for headaches was discovered over 2,000 years ago.
2. _____ Salicylic acid hurts people's stomachs.
3. _____ A primary headache may be caused by a tumor.
4. _____ Migraine sufferers have symptoms other than headache pain.
5. _____ Cluster headaches appear to be caused by stress.

B **Choose the best answer according to the reading.**

1. What was the first treatment for headaches? DETAIL
   a. Powder from the outer part of a tree
   b. Powder from tree roots
   c. Salicylic acid in liquid form
   d. Acetylsalicylic acid

2. What is the main topic of paragraph 3? TOPIC
   a. The origins of aspirin
   b. The definition of salicylic acid
   c. The process of making acetylsalicylic acid
   d. The effectiveness of aspirin for pain relief

3. In paragraph 3, the word *form* means ______. VOCABULARY
   a. size
   b. name
   c. structure
   d. category

4. What is NOT a possible cause of a primary headache? DETAIL
   a. a reduced flow of blood
   b. alcohol
   c. stress
   d. the flu

C **Fill in the blanks with information from the reading.**

1. Most people know acetylsalicylic acid as ____________________.
2. Certain ____________________ or ____________________, or other stimuli, can trigger a migraine.
3. ____________________ and ____________________ headaches usually involve pain on one side of the head.

SUMMARY

Fill in the blanks with the phrases in the box.

different triggers	another condition	weeks or months
lives and productivity	especially on migraines	from willow bark

Studying headaches is important because they affect people's
1 ______________________ worldwide.

History

- Hippocrates made a powder 2 ______________________
- Later led to the development of aspirin

Types

- Secondary: caused by 3 ______________________
- Primary:
  1) Tension headaches: caused by stress
  2) Migraine headaches: 4 ______________________
  3) Cluster headaches: happen at the same time for 5 ______________________

Future

- Study ongoing
- Progress being made, 6 ______________________

VOCABULARY PRACTICE

Fill in the blanks with the words in the box. Change the form if necessary.

physiological	tumor	productivity	stimulus	chemistry	acid

1. Lemons and similar fruits contain citric ______________, which gives them their sharp flavor.
2. Scientist are studying the ______________ of the ozone layer to help find solutions to global warming.
3. It is not clear whether the patient's pain has a psychological or ______________ cause.
4. The bump on the dog's ear is a(n) ______________, but luckily, it is not cancerous.
5. You can train an animal to respond to a certain ______________, such as the sound of a bell.
6. ______________ in the office greatly increased when the use of social-media sites was banned.

SPEAKING

4B At the Doctor's Office

A Model Conversation

Brief note

"I can't keep anything down" means you keep vomiting whenever you eat anything.

Read the conversation. Then listen. Track 22

Doctor: Hi, Robin. What seems to be the problem?

Patient: Well, doctor, I've had nausea for the last two days. I can't keep anything down.

Doctor: Have you had any other symptoms? Headache? Fever? Body aches? Anything like that?

Patient: Yes, I had a stomachache and body aches yesterday. They're gone now. I feel a little better, but I still can't eat.

Doctor: Hmm. Have you eaten any bad-tasting food recently—especially chicken, eggs, or seafood?

Patient: I don't think so. I had lunch the other day at a seafood restaurant, but the food tasted fine.

Doctor: Well, it sounds like food poisoning to me, but it's hard to know for sure. You're already getting better, so my advice is to rest and drink lots of water or juice.

Patient: You can't give me a prescription?

Doctor: Sorry, the only cure for food poisoning is time. You can buy pills for the nausea at any pharmacy, but it might not help. If your nausea isn't gone in a few days, then call me again.

B Vocabulary: Symptoms

Listen to the list of symptoms. Then write the letter of the correct definition next to each. Track 23

1. nausea ____	**a.** a high body temperature
2. sore throat ____	**b.** a feeling of sickness; wanting to vomit
3. body aches ____	**c.** having liquid come from your nose
4. cough ____	**d.** pain all over the body
5. runny nose ____	**e.** a painful feeling in your throat (inside your neck)
6. fever ____	**f.** a blocked nose; trouble breathing through your nose
7. congestion ____	**g.** getting ill from a specific thing (a food, an animal, a medication, etc.)
8. allergy ____	**h.** to push air out suddenly from your throat with a noise

C Vocabulary in Context

Listen to the words and their definitions. Practice saying the words out loud. Then fill in the blanks with the correct words. Track 24

cure: a way to stop a medical problem

food poisoning: illness from eating spoiled (not fresh) or incorrectly cooked food

gone: no longer there; (of a symptom) having stopped

pill: a small, circle-shaped piece of medication

prescription: a note from a doctor to a pharmacist about medication for a patient

1. Take one ________________ three times a day with meals.
2. The doctor gave me a ________________ for some headache medication. Now my pain is ________________!
3. There is no ________________ for a cold, but medicine can help with the symptoms.
4. Always be sure to cook chicken well, or you might get ________________.

D Grammar

Present perfect vs. Simple past

present perfect vs. simple past		
present perfect	Use the present perfect to talk about an action or state that is not finished. It has a connection to the present.	
	I**'ve lived** here for three years. (I moved here three years ago, and I still live here.)	
	Use the present perfect when the time of a past action is not important or not known.	
	I **haven't had** the flu for a long time.	We**'ve** already **seen** that movie.
simple past	Use the simple past to talk about an action or state that happened in the past and is finished.	
	I **lived** there for three years. (I do not live there anymore. I have moved.)	
	Use the simple past with past time expressions.	
	I **had** the flu **last week**, but I'm better now.	We **saw** that movie **yesterday**.

E Grammar Practice

Fill in the blanks with the correct forms of the verbs in parentheses.

1. My dad ____________________ (feel) terrible last night.
2. You ____________________ (forget) to take your pills this morning.
3. ____________________ you ever ____________________ (see) this doctor before?
4. I'm very healthy. I ____________________ (not get) sick for years!
5. She ____________________ (have) an allergy to cats since she was about 4 years old.
6. I ____________________ (take) that medicine for a week and then stopped.
7. He ____________________ (have) a severe cough yesterday, but it's gone now.
8. Maria ____________________ already ____________________ (tell) the doctor about her sore throat and body aches.

F Use the Language

I have never told a lie!

Write ten sentences about yourself. Some sentences should be true, and others should be lies. Write about things in the past, or things that started in the past and continue until now.

Then get in small groups. Share your sentences with the group. Your group will guess if your sentence is true or a lie. Each correct guess gets one point. The person with the most points at the end is the winner.

Ten things about me	
1.	**6.**
2.	**7.**
3.	**8.**
4.	**9.**
5.	**10.**

WRITING

Divide into teams of two, and choose your topic. Write your arguments on the lines below. You will argue in favor of Western medicine, or traditional Oriental medicine. Present your arguments in front of the class. Each team will have three opportunities to speak. The class will decide whose arguments were most convincing.

Team: ____

Things to Think About

Which method are people more comfortable with?
What if someone is really sick and needs surgery?
What advantages does your method have?
What are the disadvantages of the other method?
What kind of sickness/injuries can your method help best?
Is retroactive or proactive medicine better? Why?

Western medicine is better because . . .

1. ____

____

2. ____

____

3. ____

____

Traditional Oriental Medicine is better because . . .

1. ____

____

2. ____

____

3. ____

____

SUPPLEMENTAL READING

Fighting Migraines

Track 25

Aspirin works well for fighting minor headaches, but it might not be the best choice for dealing with migraines. Doctors have found that after a migraine sufferer is treated with aspirin, the person's next migraine attack may be even worse. Therefore, experts have been searching for other ways to treat these headaches.

For example, doctors have learned that certain cells in parts of the brain release proteins during a migraine attack. By using a drug that acts like the natural chemical serotonin in the brain, they can stop the cells from releasing those proteins. This has the effect of blocking the migraine.

But that is only one kind of medicine doctors have found useful in fighting migraines. It also turns out that certain anti-depressant drugs work well to relieve migraines. And surprisingly, some migraine sufferers claim Botox has proven helpful for them. (Botox is a chemical injected into the face for the purpose of reducing wrinkles.)

Not all migraine sufferers turn to medicine for help with their problem. Others use alternative remedies. Many people use yoga or meditation to relieve stress and reduce the number of migraines they suffer. And in some cases, people know that certain foods or fluorescent lights trigger their migraines. These people simply try to avoid the things that set off their migraine attacks.

Fill in the blanks with information from the reading.

1. During a migraine attack, certain parts of the brain release ____________________.
2. Anti-depressant drugs and Botox have been found to ____________________ migraines.
3. Florescent lights and certain types of food can ____________________ migraines.

EXTENSION Talk or Write About It

Do you or does anyone you know suffer from migraines? How do you/they treat them? Would you be willing to test a new headache drug that affects your brain activity? Why or why not?

UNIT 5-1 Planning Ahead

Scan for Audio

Pre-Reading Questions

◆ **Talk about these questions with your classmates.**

1. Think of your last meal. Which, if any, foods in that meal came from another country?
2. What is a benefit of foods that come from other countries?
3. What is a problem with foods that come from other countries?

VOCABULARY PREVIEW

◆ **Read the definition. Then match each word in bold with its definition.**

A. created or built long ago and still here because it is successful
B. a period of ten years
C. in the country; not near a city
D. people who buy or use things

1. ________ **Consumers** often do not know what chemicals are in the foods they buy.
2. ________ Some large cities have many **well-established** farmers' markets.
3. ________ In the US, the number of farmers' markets has grown over the past few **decades**.
4. ________ Farmers and farmers' markets are not only in **rural** area.

A Shorter Food Supply Chain

Track 26

Food chains in nature are short. Animals eat the plants that grow around them. Then other animals eat the plant-eating animals. All of the animals live in the same area.

In contrast, the food supply chain for people can be quite long. Typical ingredients or foods in a person's diet may come from halfway around the world. Such long food supply chains have certain problems. In order for the food to travel well over long distances, it might be picked before it is ripe. Or worse, it might be treated with chemicals. The accepted chemicals for use in farming or processing may differ between countries. Hence, consumers cannot always be sure what is on or in the food they get.

Because of such problems, more people are trimming their food supply chains. They are turning to locally grown or produced foods. Sometimes these locally sourced foods can be found in stores. More often, though, people "buy local" at a farmers' market. Locally sourced food items are grown or produced within 150 kilometers (km) of where they are sold or consumed.

Farmers' markets of the past were usually something like a stand or tent by a rural road. Such food outlets still exist, but they are not the typical modern farmers' market. In and around any large city, well-established farmers' markets can be found in multiple locations. In the US, the number of farmers' markets has grown a lot over the past few decades. There were around two thousand farmers' markets across the country in 1995. Today, there are nearly eight thousand.

Reading Time: ______ minutes ______ seconds 261 words

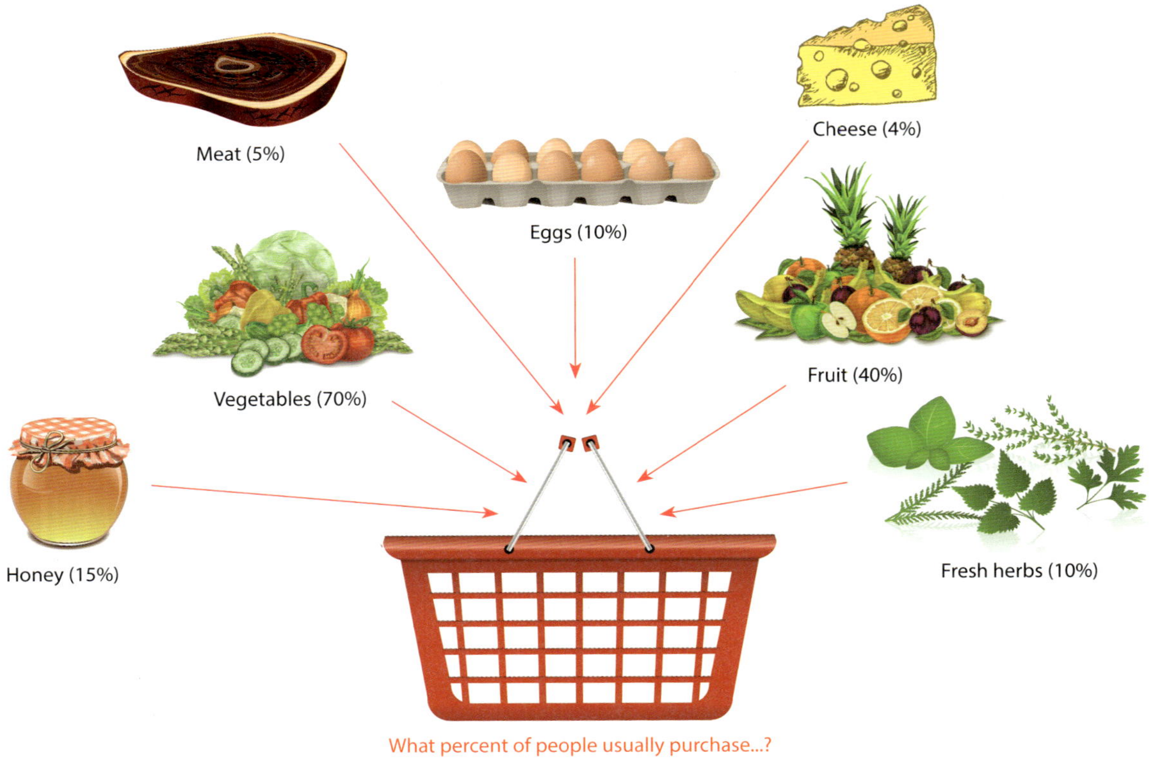

▲ Survey of shoppers at farmers' markets

Review the Highlights

◆ **Mark up the text and infographic according to the instructions.**

1. Look at Paragraphs 1 and 2. Underline the ideas that are in contrast.
2. Look at Paragraph 2. Underline the problems with long food supply chains.
3. Look at Paragraph 3. Circle the two places where locally sourced foods are found.
4. Look at Paragraph 4. Underline where farmers' markets are typically found today.
5. Look at the infographic. What does the percent in the graphic show? Check your choice:

   ☐ percentage of this food that makes up a person's diet

   ☐ percentage of this food that is grown locally

   ☐ percentage of farmers' market shoppers who often buy this item

READING COMPREHENSION

A **Circle the correct answer.**

1. What is the main topic of the reading? Main topic
   a. How people get their food
   b. What farmers prefer to grow
   c. Who eats what
   d. Why food habits differ around the world

2. Why do growers pick certain foods before they are ripe? Details: why
   a. To consume them locally
   b. To send them for sale far away
   c. To treat them with chemicals
   d. To use them as ingredients in processed food

3. Why does the writer mention stands and tents in the reading? Purpose
   a. To describe old style farmers' markets
   b. To explain common outlets today
   c. To illustrate a short food supply chain
   d. To suggest the best place for shopping

4. According to the passage and the infographic, which food item is NOT usually bought from farmers' markets? Negative fact
   a. Bread
   b. Eggs
   c. Honey
   d. Vegetables

5. Where can farmers' markets probably be found, according to the reading? Inference
   a. Around typical modern homes
   b. Far from a rural road
   c. Inside a supermarket
   d. Within a big city

B **Complete the summary. Write the words from the reading that best fit in the blanks. One word is extra.**

decades chains well-established tent rural consumer kilometers items

Food 1. ______________ for animals and those for people differ in that people can get their food from all over the world. Many problems are caused by the long food chains created by 2. ______________ demand. For one thing, certain food 3. ______________ may be picked and shipped to stores or outlets before they are ripe. Or worse, these foods might be treated with chemicals so that they can travel over many 4. ______________. Due to these problems, people are looking for ways to improve their food supply chains. One way to do this is to "buy local" in a farmers' market. The number of farmers' markets has grown a lot over the past few 5. ______________. Farmers' markets in the past were usually 6. ______________, but today, 7. ______________ farmers' markets can be found in and around big cities.

SUMMARY

1. Work in pairs or in small groups. Read the list of fruits below. Together, try to list three countries where these fruits are probably grown as a major crop.

 Avocados: ____________, ____________, ____________

 Mangos: ____________, ____________, ____________

 Papayas: ____________, ____________, ____________

 Pineapples: ____________, ____________, ____________

2. Read the information below related to these fruit crops. As you read, circle any countries you listed above.

We are lucky today that we can enjoy tropical fruits all year around. Of all tropical fruits sold in stores, four kinds make up 75% of all tropical fruits sold. These four "major tropical fruits" are mango, pineapple, papaya, and avocado. More than 60 million tons are grown every year. More than 90% of all this fruit is grown in developing countries.

The most popular of the major tropical fruits are mangos. More than thirty million tons are grown every year. The countries growing the most mangos include China, Thailand, the Philippines, and India.

After mangos, pineapples are the second most popular tropical fruit. About 16 million tons of this fruit are grown each year. The Philippines, Thailand, Brazil, and Costa Rica are all major pineapple producers.

Papayas come in third in the tropical fruit all-star list with about twelve million tons grown per year. The top papaya-growing countries are India, Brazil, and Nigeria.

After papaya, avocados rank as the fourth most popular tropical fruit. Around three million tons of this fruit are grown and sold each year. Mexico grows by far the most of this fruit. It is followed by Chile and the Dominican Republic.

VOCABULARY PRACTICE

Fill in the blanks with the words in the box. Change the form if necessary.

multiple	number	differ	ingredient	contrast

1. In ____________, the food supply chain for people can be quite long.
2. Typical ____________ or foods in a person's diet may come from halfway around the world.
3. The accepted chemicals for use in farming or processing may ____________ between countries.
4. Well-established farmers' markets can be found in ____________ locations.
5. In the US, the ____________ of farmers' markets has grown a lot over the past few decades.

5A I'll Take the Non-stop Flight

A Model Conversation

Read the conversation. Then listen. Track 27

Helen: Hey, Paulo, I'm booking the flights for us and Dana. Do you want to check the information first?

Paulo: Okay. So, you're booking three round-trip tickets to New York, right?

Helen: Right.

Paulo: There are a lot of airports in New York City. Which one is our destination?

Helen: LaGuardia.

Paulo: And we're departing on the 28th? Hmm. I don't know…

Helen: Is that a problem?

Paulo: It's a Friday. Airfares are more expensive on weekends. If we fly on Wednesday or Thursday, it would be cheaper.

Helen: I know, but the flights available on those days are fully booked.

Paulo: Ah, okay. I see there's a three-hour layover. How much are the direct flights?

Helen: They start at $70 more.

Paulo: That's not too bad. If it means we don't have to wait three hours for a connection, I think it's worth it.

Helen: Okay. I'll book this one. Three economy-class tickets. Do you want a window or aisle seat?

Paulo: I'll take the aisle.

Brief note

"Economy class" is sometimes called coach.

B Vocabulary

Match each word or phrase with the correct definition.

1. round-trip	**a.** a stop during a long trip
2. direct/non-stop	**b.** the cheapest kind of seat on a plane
3. layover	**c.** without stopping
4. airfare	**d.** to leave to go on a trip or journey
5. connection	**e.** traveling to a place and back
6. economy class	**f.** the place you are going to
7. depart	**g.** when you get off one flight and onto another
8. destination	**h.** the cost of an airplane ticket

C Vocabulary Comprehension

Fill in the blanks with the correct words from above.

Hi, Dana.

Paulo and I booked three ❶ ____________ tickets for New York, leaving on the 28th! I'm emailing your e-ticket to you. Good news—it's a ❷ ____________ flight. There was a cheaper flight with a ❸ ____________, but it's better to fly non-stop. And the ❹ ____________ for that other flight was only $70 less.

You'll also be happy to know that Paulo is taking the ❺ ____________ ____________, so you can have the window seat. Looking forward to the trip!

Best,
Helen

D Grammar

Second conditional

second conditional

Second conditional sentences are *if* sentences about a hypothetical (unreal) situation. The first conditional is about something that is probable in the future. The second conditional is about something that is not true in the present or something that is less probable in the future.

Second conditional sentences have the form *If* + subject + simple past verb phrase, (*then*) subject + *would* + verb phrase.

if **clause: condition**	***would*** **clause: result**	**(+ extra information)**
If I **were** rich,	I **would** / I**'d travel** around the world.	(I'm not rich.)
If she **took** a relaxing trip,	then her health **would get** better.	(She has no plans to take a trip.)
If we **didn't have** exams next week,	we **would** / we**'d stay** in Mexico longer.	(We do have exams next week.)

The *would* clause can come first. No comma is needed in this case.

I**'d travel** around the world if I **were** rich.
My friends **would be** upset if we **missed** our connection.

Brief note

In the second conditional, the use of *were* with singular subjects is considered correct: *If I/he/she **were** rich, ...*
But it's okay to use *was* informally: *If I/he/she **was** rich, ...*

Brief note

In the result clause, you can use *could* instead of *would* to talk about possibilities: *If we **didn't have** exams next week, we **could stay** in Mexico longer.*

E Grammar Practice

Circle the correct answers.

1. (Whether / If) they took the train, the trip would take much longer.
2. If I could travel anywhere, I would probably (go / going) to France.
3. If Robert (didn't / doesn't) have to work today, he could drive you to the airport.
4. If I (were / would be) in a window seat, I'd be able to sleep.
5. I would definitely fly Korean Air if I (had / have) a choice.
6. Jenny wouldn't get angry if her sister's flight (arriving / arrived) late.
7. Our flight to London (was / would be) cheaper if we traveled on a weekday.

F Use the Language

Booking a flight

You and your partner are planning to take a trip. First, agree on a destination. Then write a conversation in which you are calling to book a flight. Perform your conversation for the class.

WRITING

1. What is your plan for your next vacation?

2. What is your favorite place to travel to in Korea?

SUPPLEMENTAL READING

Tabula Rasa

Track 28

When you enter the main building of Keimyung University, a blank canvas is hanging in the front lobby, with the title 'Tabula Rasa' in Latin. 'Tabula Rasa' means 'blank slate.' This concept means we can shape our future. It encourages students not to be afraid of challenges and to cultivate their own future with confidence. It serves as a daily reminder that every decision, every action, and every opportunity is a chance to create the future they desire.

Keimyung University has encouraged students to embrace the FACE qualities: Frontier Spirit, Altruistic Service Mind, Cultural Sensitivity, and Expertise. Now is the time for Keimyung University students to leave their mark on the canvas of Tabula Rasa. Stay positive, embrace each challenge with a can-do attitude, and never forget that every step forward is progress. With determination and passion, they have the power to shape not just their own future, but the future of the world around them.

EXTENSION Talk or Write About It

1. What does the idea of a 'blank slate' or 'Tabula Rasa' mean to you? How can it help students in their university life?
2. What do you desire for your future? How will you achieve your goals?
3. Do you think people are born with their talents; or do they learn them from their family and environment? Why do you think so?

UNIT 5-2 Planning Ahead

Scan for Audio

Pre-Reading Questions

◆ **Think about the following questions.**

1. Would you like to travel to space? What would you do while you were there?
2. Do you think sending people to the Moon again should be a priority? Why or why not?
3. Why do you think governments spend so much money exploring space?

VOCABULARY PREVIEW

◆ **Match each word with the correct definition.**

1. shuttle	a. woven or knitted material
2. fabric	b. relating to light or the ability to see
3. quantum	c. a difference or disagreement between two things which means both cannot be true
4. optical	d. a vehicle that travels back and forth between places
5. missile	e. the smallest amount of energy that can be measured
6. contradiction	f. a flying weapon that can travel a long distance before exploding at the place at which it is aimed

WHY GO INTO SPACE?

Track 29

Why do humans feel the need to explore space? The reasons are various, from the **abstract**[1] to the military, from the scientific to the economic. Often, these motives sit in direct **contradiction** to each other, and while exploring space has obvious benefits, it also carries great risks.

A major historic reason for space exploration has been national pride. Governments like those of the US and USSR used achievements in space to display power. They also suggested that children would be inspired, and humankind would gain a new sense of its own potential. Certainly, the 1969 Apollo Moon landing captured the imagination, but it has not been repeated since 1972. When asked in 2019, only one-third of US citizens believed it was a priority to send humans to the Moon again. However, when asked if the US should maintain its role as a leader in space, seventy-two percent said that it should. Why? First, space is an important arena for national security. Satellite systems give early warning of **incoming**[2] **missiles** and ensure the accuracy of **outgoing**[3] attacks. On top of this, satellites **intercept**[4] emails and phone or radio communications from suspected criminals and terrorists.

Q What did governments say space exploration would do for children?

On the other hand, for some citizens, the ability to go to war and monitor private communications may not count as a benefit. And, while the Outer Space Treaty of 1967 makes it illegal to put weapons into space, the UN is concerned that it may be out-of-date and that the accumulation of space weapons in the future is highly likely. Another drawback of space exploration is its cost. In total, the US government has spent $650 billion on NASA projects. Opponents argue that this is money that could have been spent helping people out of poverty, fighting climate change, and addressing other problems on our home planet.

Supporters of space exploration respond that space science has brought us extremely valuable knowledge that benefits humankind. We now have a deeper scientific understanding of **quantum** physics, the solar system, and the Sun. Researchers have learned about solar wind

1 **abstract** *adj.* existing as an idea, feeling, or quality, not as a material object
2 **incoming** *adj.* arriving at or coming toward a place
3 **outgoing** *adj.* leaving a place
4 **intercept** *v.* to stop something as it goes to a particular place

What is the collective name for solar wind and solar flares?

and **solar flares**[5]. These phenomena, known as space weather, can have direct effects on human life as they interfere with satellites and can even cause power cuts on Earth. From space, we can also monitor and understand the weather on our own planet. Further, satellites also allow us to use the Global Positioning System (GPS) and safely navigate around the world. This all leaves us better placed to ensure the safety of the Earth's population. Space research has led to many other technological **breakthroughs**[6] that help humans every day. Without it, we would not have artificial arms and legs, **optical** lenses that cannot be scratched, heat-resistant **fabric** for firefighters' suits, shock absorbers for buildings at risk from earthquakes, tablets that clean water, CT scans that find diseases, freeze-dried food, or even the computer mouse.

What did the *Challenger* and *Columbia* incidents lead to?

a. A lack of public interest in NASA's projects
b. The closure of one of NASA's projects

Not all advancements from space exploration are accidental **by-products**[7], though. In-Space Manufacturing (ISM) involves making or growing things in the space environment, including metals, medicines, and even human organs. The lack of gravity makes mixing elements easier, and working in a **vacuum**[8] ensures the materials are incredibly pure. Still, ISM requires a human crew, and the dangers of manned missions remain high. The *Challenger* and *Columbia* space **shuttle** disasters, which killed seven US astronauts each in 1986 and 2003, made many question whether sending humans into space was worth it. Eventually, it led to the end of the space shuttle program. Today, much space science is done remotely by robots; this lacks the drama of watching astronauts blast off, but at least the public knows it won't end in tragedy.

The results of exploring space are varied and complex. Some are positive and concrete, like life-saving inventions. Others are frightening but hard to measure, like the threat of a weapons **buildup**[9] in space. This important debate will likely continue indefinitely among scientists, policy-makers, and the public.

Reading Time: _______ minutes _______ seconds 652 words

5	**solar flare**	*n.*	a sudden temporary outburst of energy from a small area of the Sun's surface
6	**breakthrough**	*n.*	an important discovery that helps to improve a situation or provide an answer to a problem
7	**by-product**	*n.*	something that is unexpectedly produced while making or doing something else
8	**vacuum**	*n.*	a space from which almost all matter (solids, liquids, gases) has been removed
9	**buildup**	*n.*	an increase in something that occurs as time passes

READING COMPREHENSION

A **Mark each statement as true (T) or false (F) according to the reading.**

1. ______ Humans haven't visited the Moon since the 1970s.
2. ______ Space weapons have been legal since the 1960s.
3. ______ Space research could help us solve climate change, according to supporters.
4. ______ Space weather can make it difficult to use electronic devices on Earth.
5. ______ Robots carry out most ISM work.

B **Choose the best answer according to the reading.**

1. What is the main idea of the reading? MAIN IDEA
   a. Countries must go into space to ensure their national security.
   b. The strongest motivation to explore space is technological advancement.
   c. Space exploration has probably accomplished all that it can.
   d. There are persuasive reasons both for and against going into space.

2. Which is NOT true according to paragraph 2? DETAIL
   a. Space travel was a source of patriotism during the 20th century.
   b. Most Americans think it's important to go back to the Moon.
   c. A presence in space can give countries a military advantage.
   d. Satellites can be useful in preventing crime and terrorism.

3. What can be inferred about the UN from paragraph 3? INFERENCE
   a. It strongly opposed the 1967 Outer Space Treaty.
   b. It most likely prefers NASA to lead space exploration.
   c. It probably supports an updated space treaty.
   d. It hopes to control any future weapons in space.

4. The word *they* in paragraph 4 refers to ______. REFERENCE
   a. phenomena
   b. effects
   c. researchers
   d. satellites

C **Look for the answers in the reading and write them on the lines.**

1 Name two space-research breakthroughs that protect humans from danger or disease.

____

2 What are the benefits of ISM?

____

SUMMARY

Fill in the blanks with the phrases in the box.

useful by-products	motivate nations	accidental and intended
sterile environment	navigate safely	national pride

There are a number of factors that 1 ______________________ to explore space. During the Cold War, both the US and USSR used advances in space as a way to boost 2 ______________________. Having a presence in space is also seen as crucial to ensuring national security. Space exploration has also brought both 3 ______________________ benefits to humankind more generally. Satellites constantly monitor the weather on Earth and allow us to 4 ______________________ using GPS. Space research led to the creation of 5 ______________________, such as artificial limbs and freeze-dried food. More recently, researchers have developed In-Space Manufacturing to create things humans need in a(n) 6 ______________________.

VOCABULARY PRACTICE

Fill in the blanks with the words in the box. Change the form if necessary.

contradiction	fabric	optical	quantum	missile	shuttle

1. The hotel ________________ takes guests to the airport every fifteen minutes.
2. The study of how tiny particles behave is called ________________ mechanics.
3. When Jen said she hated junk food but enjoyed hamburgers, Lisa pointed out that it was a(n) ________________.
4. The fighter jet fired five ________________ at the bridge in order to destroy it.
5 Cotton is one of the most popular ________________ for clothes because it is inexpensive, washable, and comfortable.
6 Dr. Harris is an expert on ________________ health; he often tells people that it is important not to look at computer screens for too long.

SPEAKING

5B Hotel or Motel?

A Model Monologue

Read the monologue. Then listen. Discuss the questions below with a partner. Track 30

Brad: My brother Jim and I are planning to take a vacation together and drive across the country. We'll stop overnight in a few cities on the way, but we cannot agree on where to stay. I want to save money and stay in inexpensive motel rooms. A comfortable double room with air-conditioning is good enough for me. We could check out early in the morning, buy food at the supermarket, and then continue driving. We used to do this on family trips when we were children.

Jim prefers to book nice hotel suites with lots of amenities. He has stayed in many nice hotels because of his old job. When he traveled for his job, he would swim in the pool, exercise in the gym, order room service, and eat in the hotel restaurant. He says he wouldn't mind the expense, but I think it's silly to waste so much money on a one-night stay.

Discuss

1. What are the benefits of staying in a hotel? A motel?
2. Which one would you prefer, a hotel or a motel?

B Vocabulary

Listen to Jim making a reservation. Fill in the blanks with the correct words and phrases from the box. (Three will not be used.) Track 31

vacation	overnight	comfortable	suite	double room
air-conditioning	amenities	inexpensive	room service	check out

1. Jim chooses to book a(n) ____________ ____________ rather than a(n) ____________.
2. They will stay ____________ and ____________ ____________ on June 15th.
3. The room comes with many ____________, including air-conditioning and ____________ ____________.
4. Internet service at the hotel is not free, but it's pretty ____________.

C In Your World

Tell your partner about a hotel or motel you have stayed in. Say whether you would recommend it or not, and explain why. Take notes on your partner's experience and describe it to the class.

D Grammar

would and *used to*

Brief note

Used to can also be used to talk about past states, with stative verbs such as *be, have, like, own,* etc. *Would* cannot be used with stative verbs.
(✓) *My hair **used to be** long. / She **used to have** a dog.*
(X) *My hair would be long. / She would have a dog.*

would* and *used to		
Both *would* + verb and *used to* + verb can be used to talk about habits or repeated actions in the past. They describe things that often or regularly happened in the past, but no longer happen.		
statement	My grandmother **would bake** cookies for us. We **would travel** to Guadalajara in the spring.	Sean **used to stay** at a hotel in London. The Faber family **used to fly** to Italy once a year.
negative	We **wouldn't** usually **take** expensive trips. I **wouldn't shop** much when I was on vacation.	That hotel **didn't use to charge** a parking fee! We **didn't use to travel** in the summer when we were kids.
question	**Would** they **drive** all night or stop at a motel? Where **would** you **go** on those long bike rides?	**Did** she **use to book** a room in advance or just show up? What **did** you **use to do** on weekends?

Brief note

In negatives and questions using the auxiliary verb *do*, the correct form is *use to*.

E Grammar Practice

Read the article. Fill in the blanks with *would* or *used to* and the correct form of the given verb. (For some blanks, more than one answer is possible.)

The History of Motels

Highways ❶ ________________ (were) rare in North America until the 1920s. Before then, people ❷ ________________ (didn't take) long car trips often. When they did go on long trips, they ❸ ________________ (slept) in their cars.

In the 1920s, highways became more common. Smart businesspeople ❹ ________________ (built) small, simple hotels near highways for travelers. These hotels were called motor hotels, or motels. The owners ❺ ________________ (put) free parking spaces right next to the rooms.

Motels ❻ ________________ (were) even more popular than they are today. They were most popular in the 1950s and 1960s. Most motels ❼ ________________ (were owned) by one person or family. Now most of them are owned by big companies.

F Listen to Speak

Listen to the conversation between a motel clerk and a customer. Then read the statements and circle true or false. Track 32

1.	The man's family used to visit the Green Lake Motel.	true	false
2.	The man would go swimming in the motel pool in the past.	true	false
3.	The motel didn't use to have a restaurant.	true	false
4.	As a kid, the man would enjoy the view of the lake.	true	false
5.	The motel's amenities now include breakfast and boat rental.	true	false
6.	The man decides to book one double room for one night.	true	false

Now role-play a telephone conversation with a partner. You are making a motel or hotel booking, and you have questions about the types of rooms available, amenities, and costs. Take turns being the customer and the motel or hotel clerk.

WRITING

1. If you have a chance to visit a foreign country, where would you want to go?

2. Do you think countries should spend money on research for space travel?

SUPPLEMENTAL READING

Cassini-Huygens: Working Together

Track 33

Although space exploration has the ability to divide nations, some missions have the opposite effect: they bring people from all over the world together.

One such mission was the *Cassini-Huygens* project, on which twenty-eight countries worked together to design and build a robotic spacecraft capable of traveling to Saturn. *Cassini*, the main spacecraft, was built by NASA in the USA, while *Huygens*—a smaller "passenger" on *Cassini*—was built by the European Space Agency (ESA).

One of the main objectives of the mission was to investigate Saturn's mysterious rings. However, scientists also wanted to find out whether Saturn—or one of its eighty-two moons—could support life. So, in 1997, *Cassini-Huygens* was launched from Cape Canaveral, USA, and began its seven-year journey to Saturn.

In July 2004, the spacecraft entered Saturn's orbit and began sending data and images back to Earth. Later that year, Saturn's moon, Titan, passed close to the planet and *Huygens*'s moment had come. It left *Cassini* and began a two-and-a-half-hour descent to the surface of Titan. With parachutes to soften its landing, it found solid ground and sent 350 images of the moon's surface back to Earth via *Cassini*.

Back on Earth, over 260 scientists from seventeen different countries waited to receive the images, as well as data from the mission as a whole. They found that Saturn's rings are made of ice and rock and are quite new, having been formed while dinosaurs were still living on Earth. They were also surprised to find an ocean and rivers of water on Titan; these may even support life.

The mission was so successful that it was extended until, after a twenty-year mission, *Cassini* was destroyed in 2017 while entering Saturn's atmosphere. It leaves behind a more detailed knowledge of our solar system and a reminder of what can be achieved when nations work together.

Fill in the blanks with information from the reading.

1. The ______________________ *Cassini-Huygens* was the result of collaboration between many nations.
2. *Cassini-Huygens* entered Saturn's ______________________ seven years after it launched.
3. *Huygens* used ______________________ to slowly descend to the surface of Titan.

EXTENSION Talk or Write About It

What do you think are the biggest benefits of exploring space? What are the biggest drawbacks? Which parts of space exploration do you think governments should prioritize?

UNIT 6-1 Shopping

Pre-Reading Questions

◆ **Talk about these questions with your classmates.**

1. Which color in the picture do you like the most?
2. Why do you like it the most?
3. How does it make you feel?

Scan for Audio

VOCABULARY PREVIEW

◆ **Read the definition. Then match each word in bold with its definition.**

A. supporting something or someone for a long time
B. to cause to like or be interested in something
C. a large building with many different shops inside
D. a feeling
E. tight; not flexible; unable to stretch
F. safe; protected
G. the feeling that something is very important and needs immediate attention
H. a small folding case that holds money, credit cards, etc.

1. ________ Different colors can bring out certain **emotions** in us.
2. ________ The color blue can make shoppers feel **loyal** to stores.
3. ________ **Malls** are very colorful places.
4. ________ Stores try to get shoppers to open their **wallets**.
5. ________ The color pink makes people feel calm and relaxes **tense** muscles.
6. ________ Some colors are known to make people feel **secure**.
7. ________ Red **attracts** customers, but it may also make them feel tense.
8. ________ The color red is related to a sense of **urgency**.

Do Colors Make You Spend More?

Track 34

If you walk into any mall, you will notice a rainbow of different colors. It is well known that colors affect our emotions. Stores often use this knowledge to influence how shoppers spend their money. In fact, there are even experts who help stores use color to make people spend more.

Experts have taught stores a variety of ways to get shoppers to open their wallets. Black makes things look classy. Many makeup products are packaged in black so that shoppers who buy them will feel special. Purple reminds people of royalty, and it is also used to package beauty products. It makes the buyer believe

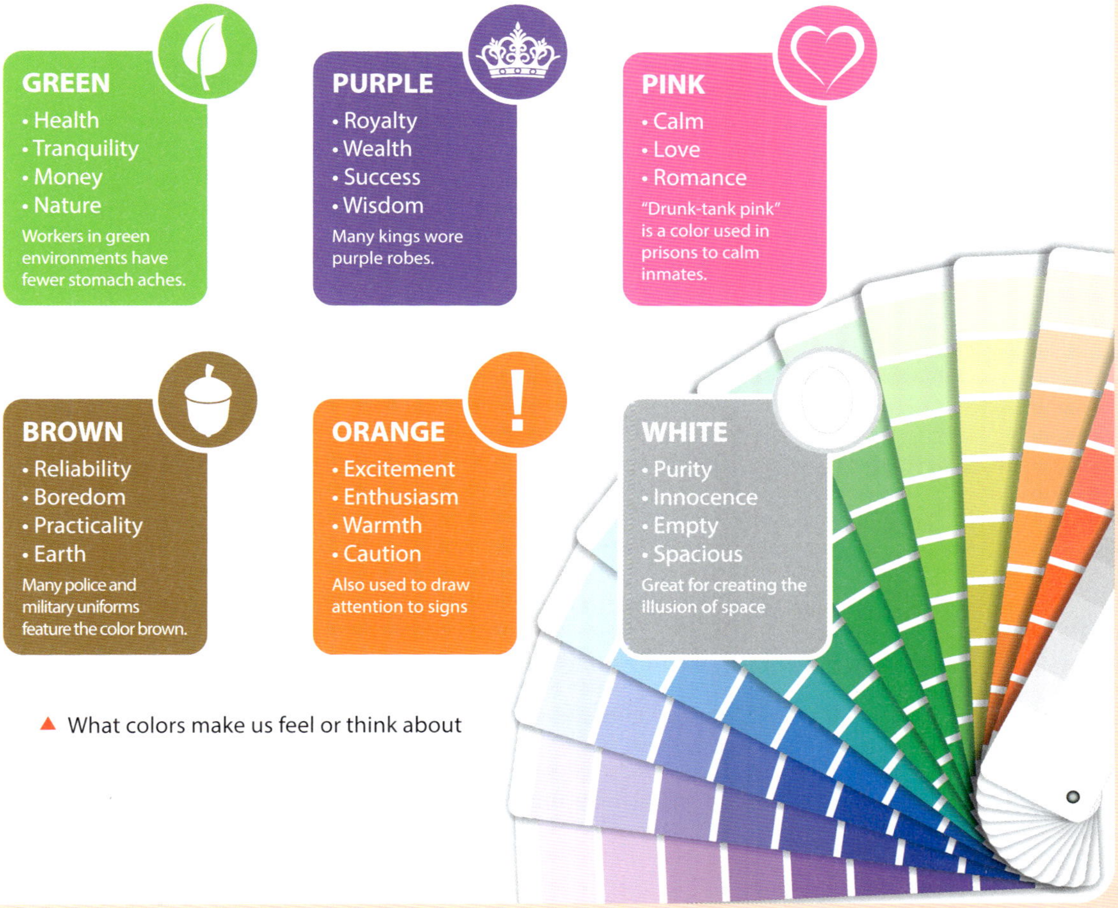

▲ What colors make us feel or think about

the item is important.

Other colors make people feel safe. For example, blue makes people feel secure. This is why many banks have blue logos. It also makes customers more loyal. White is similar. It brings out feelings of honesty and purity.

Pink makes people feel calm. It is known to help relax tense muscles. Red, however, has the opposite reaction. Although red may attract customers, it is related to a sense of urgency. This is why many clearance sale signs are red.

Bright colors, such as green and orange, have positive effects on people. Green makes people think about nature and doing good things for the planet. Orange makes shoppers feel that something is a good value. Fast food logos are often orange because buyers feel they are getting more food for their money.

No matter where you shop, it is important to be aware before opening your wallet. By knowing how colors are used, people can prevent stores from controlling how they spend their money.

Reading Time: _______ minutes _______ seconds   273 words

Review the Highlights

◆ **Mark up the text and infographic according to the instructions.**

1. Look at Paragraph 1. Underline what thing stores use to influence people to spend their money.
2. Look at Paragraph 2. Circle what purple makes buyers believe.
3. Look at Paragraph 3. Underline what color banks use for their logos.
4. Look at the infographic. Besides calm, circle two other emotions people relate with pink.
5. Look at the infographic. Underline what people think of when they see green.

READING COMPREHENSION

A **Circle the correct answer.**

1. How do experts help stores bring in more money? Details: how
   a. They package products in red.
   b. They use color to influence how shoppers spend money.
   c. They help customers feel calm.
   d. They make buyers feel like they are getting more for their money.

2. Why does white make people feel more loyal? Details: why
   a. Because it makes people feel calm.
   b. Because it makes people feel classy.
   c. Because it brings out feelings of honesty.
   d. Because it brings out a sense of urgency.

3. What is the reading about? Main idea
   a. Colors that make people feel safe and calm.
   b. Why many clearance sale signs are red.
   c. How color affects what people do and how they feel.
   d. Different ways to get shoppers to open their wallets.

4. According to the text, which color is NOT always related to a positive emotion? Negative fact
   a. Pink b. White c. Black d. Red

5. Based on the reading, how can you keep from spending money? Main situation
   a. Be aware that black can make you feel special.
   b. Only buy clearance items.
   c. Be aware of how stores use color to make you open your wallet.
   d. Do not go into stores with blue logos.

B **Complete the summary. Write the words from the reading that best fit in the blanks. One word is extra.**

tense attract wallets mall emotions loyal urgency secure

When you go to a 1. ______________, you will see many different colors. These colors can change your 2. ______________. Experts know how to use colors to get shoppers to open their 3. ______________. Banks use colors, such as blue, that make people feel 4. ______________ and 5. ______________. Pink makes people feel less 6. ______________. Red can make people feel a sense of 7. ______________. Experts know that people are attracted to certain colors. However, it is up to you to know how to prevent stores from controlling how you spend your money.

SUMMARY

1. **Work with a partner. Ask your partner which emotions he or she associates with each color. Next, discuss the stores, brands, and logos that use those colors. Switch roles.**

Color	**Emotions** - How do these colors make you feel?	**Stores/Brands/Logos** - Which stores, brands, or logos use these colors?
Red		
Orange		
Yellow		
Green		
Blue		
Purple		
Pink		
White		
Black		

2. **Discuss the following questions with your partner.**

1. What is your favorite color? What was your favorite color as a child? Has your favorite color changed as you have gotten older? Why do you think that is?
2. Is there a color you hate? If so, what is it? Why do you hate it?

3. **Choose one of the topics below. Write a paragraph about it.**

1. Do you think different cultures have different meanings for colors? What do the different colors mean in your culture? Provide examples to support your answer.

____

____

2. What colors are in your country's flag? What do the colors represent?

____

____

VOCABULARY PRACTICE

Fill in the blanks with the words in the box. Change the form if necessary.

aware	remind	affect	value	positive

1. It is well known that colors ________________ our emotions.
2. Purple ________________ people of royalty.
3. Bright colors have ________________ effects on people.
4. Orange makes shoppers feel that something is a good ________________.
5. It is important to be ________________ before opening your wallet.

SPEAKING

6A The Best Shopping in Town

A Authentic Text: Shopping guide

Read part of a tourist information brochure about shopping in San Francisco. Which of these places would you most like to visit?

SAN FRANCISCO SHOPPING GUIDE

1 North Beach

Don't miss out on San Francisco's well-known Italian district, with an *Italiano* style that you can see and taste! Visit fashionable shops offering clothing, accessories, and home décor. And when you're done, enjoy authentic Italian food at one of the many fine restaurants in the area.

2 Union Square

This downtown district is the number-one destination for both local shoppers and tourists. Shop around for men's and women's clothing, accessories, beauty products, electronics, and more. If you ever get tired of shopping, you can check out some of Union Square's many theaters, art galleries, salons, or hotels.

3 Chinatown

Not far from North Beach, there's a little piece of China. You will feel like you're in Shanghai as you explore shops with a huge selection of imports, from furniture to tea. From the area's many street vendors, you can also pick up fun souvenirs and some delicious but inexpensive Chinese cuisine.

B Vocabulary

Match the words and phrases with the correct definitions.

1. accessory	•	• **a.**	brought from one country to another for sale
2. electronics	•	• **b.**	a certain area or neighborhood in a city
3. get tired of	•	• **c.**	something you buy to remember a place you visited
4. district	•	• **d.**	a number of different choices
5. genuine	•	• **e.**	products that use electricity, such as TVs, computers, cell phones, etc.
6. fashionable	•	• **f.**	cooking; food
7. selection	•	• **g.**	something you wear besides clothes, such as a hat, a scarf, a bag, etc.
8. imported	•	• **h.**	showing taste and style (in clothes, hair, etc.) that is popular now
9. souvenir	•	• **i.**	real; true; not copied or false
10. cuisine	•	• **j.**	to become bored or impatient with (something)

C About You

Think of the last time you visited a popular shopping area. What was it like? Did you buy anything? Tell a partner, and answer his or her questions. Listen to your partner's experience and ask questions.

D Grammar

Phrasal verbs

Brief note

Inseparable phrasal verbs may be transitive (having a direct object) or intransitive. All separable phrasal verbs are transitive.

phrasal verbs		
Phrasal verbs are made up of a verb plus one or more particles (words that look like prepositions or adverbs): for example, *hang out*. Phrasal verbs are most common in informal speech and writing. There are two main types: inseparable and separable.		
	examples	**sentences**
inseparable There is no object between the verb and the particle(s).	*hang out, drop by, get around, shop around (for), miss out (on), log in/out, sign in/out*	Let's **hang out** at the mall. Don't **miss out on** this amazing sale. I want to **shop around for** phones before I buy one. **Drop by** our store to get a great deal on shoes.
separable The object may come between the verb and the particle.	*turn on/off, pick up, think over, throw away, look up, find out, check out, put on, take off, drop off*	Did you **pick up** some school supplies? Did you **pick** them **up**? We should **check** Chinatown **out** before we go. We should **check** it **out** before we go.

Brief note

When the object is a personal pronoun, it must come between the verb and the particle.
(✓) ***Pick** it **up***. (X) *Pick up it*.

E Grammar Practice

Fill in the blanks with one of the phrasal verbs from above. Use a dictionary to help you if necessary.

1. My mom used to ________________ me ________________ at school every morning.
2. I'm going to ________________ my shoes ________________ because they're uncomfortable.
3. It's getting cold. You should ________________ ________________ your sweater.
4. If you don't come to the party, you'll ________________ ________________ ________________ a fun evening.

Underline the error and write the correct phrase.

5. I didn't know the meaning of this word, so I looked up it. ____________________
6. He uses the subway to get town around. ____________________
7. No one is watching TV, so please turn off it. ____________________
8. My parents are out of town. Want to hang it out? ____________________

F Use the Language

Partners in business

Working in pairs or small groups, pick a business, store, or restaurant that you are familiar with. Discuss the details of this business, including the following:

- Its name
- Its location
- The kind of food/products it sells
- Its pricing (expensive or inexpensive)
- Its selling points (how it's different and why people will like it)

Then write a radio advertisement (5–7 sentences) for the business, store, or restaurant you chose. One partner will read your advertisement to the class. Both or all partners should be ready to answer questions from your classmates!

____

____

____

____

____

____

____

WRITING

1. Do you prefer online shopping or offline shopping? Why?

SUPPLEMENTAL READING

Dongsan Library

Track 35

As of September 1, 2023, Dongsan Library holds 1,351,451 domestic books and 346,672 foreign books, amounting to 85.3 books per student. The library also houses a diverse collection of classical Chinese (Hanmun) texts, including nationally designated cultural properties (treasures) and Daegu city tangible cultural assets. Among universities in South Korea, Keimyung University holds the second-largest collection of national cultural heritage items, after Seoul National University's Kyujanggak.

In May 2022, to commemorate the 123rd anniversary of Keimyung University, Dongsan Library established the Rare Bible Room to display valuable materials such as Bibles and prayer books. This collection includes a Latin Bible published in 1580, along with ancient Hebrew and Greek Bibles and prayer books. Additionally, it features Bibles, prayer books, liturgical books, and sermon collections in various languages, including English, German, Italian, French, Spanish, Russian, Welsh, Swedish, Czech, and Korean.

Source: 빛을 여는 계명인. 계명대학교 출판부. 2024. p.250–259.

EXTENSION Talk or Write About It

1. How often do you go to Dongsan Library?
2. What do you usually do there?
3. Have you viewed assets at any of the special exhibits at Dongsan Library?

UNIT 6-2 Shopping

Scan for Audio

Pre-Reading Questions

◆ **Think about the following questions.**

1. How much exercise do you do every day? How do you measure it?
2. Would wearing a fitness tracker motivate you to exercise? Why or why not?
3. What are the advantages of fitness trackers? Are there any disadvantages?

VOCABULARY PREVIEW

◆ **Match each word with the correct definition.**

1. feedback •	• a. using a careful system or method
2. indicator •	• b. a sign of something
3. elaborate •	• c. information regarding performance
4. systematic •	• d. the heartbeat as it is felt elsewhere in the body
5. quantitative •	• e. of or relating to measurement in numbers
6. pulse •	• f. complicated; sophisticated

Wearable Fitness Trackers

Track 36

In June of 2015, Fitbit CEO James Park had something worth keeping track of besides his footsteps. The Fitbit initial public offering (IPO) was among the strongest of the year. The company's stock prices soared in the first hours of trading and retained their value after the **hype**[1] wore off. Fitbit was at the forefront of a new wave of health and fitness products: fitness trackers.

Electronic fitness trackers are a cross between medical biometric devices like the EKG machine, which tracks the heart's electrical activity, and a personal trainer. Based in part on the motion sensors in gaming controllers, the devices and their accompanying software can track a range of variables. These include steps taken, floors climbed, **pulse** rate, calories burned, hours spent standing, and hours spent sleeping restfully. Fitness trackers can even provide encouragement. The Fitbit **platform**[2], for instance, awards "**badges**[3]" to users when they reach certain milestones, such as losing five pounds. These devices promise users a more precise and **systematic** way to pursue their goals.

What do fitness trackers have in common with gaming controllers?

Trackers are becoming increasingly popular. A 2020 Pew Research Center survey found that one-fifth of adults polled use them as part of their exercise routine. And initial evidence suggests they may really help. The basic concept of counting steps has been around for quite a while with the pedometer, a simple electronic device that performs only that

[1] **hype** *n.* talk or writing intended to make people excited about something; publicity
[2] **platform** *n.* an operating system
[3] **badge** *n.* a small object awarded for a particular accomplishment

function. Although fitness trackers have more **elaborate** features, they all include pedometers. Counting steps is a sort of exercise supervision. Researchers at a London university conducted a years-long study on the effectiveness of keeping track of steps. One group of subjects did not use fitness trackers, while the other did. After four years, the fitness-tracker group did more exercise and had a lower risk of **fractures**[4], heart attacks, and strokes.

What health issue has been connected to fitness-tracker sales?

Recent data on the dangers of **sedentary**[5] lifestyles may also be driving sales. Because sitting still on the job causes health problems that are irreversible even with regular exercise, many are enlisting the help of fitness trackers. Counting steps and floors climbed at work can help users consciously increase the total amount of movement per day and **counteract**[6] the effects of sitting still in front of a screen.

However, there is by no means an expert consensus on the accuracy of the other types of data that fitness trackers claim to record. Critics have doubts that such a device can correctly measure the number of calories burned. They **point out**[7] that it cannot possibly take into account important aspects of a person's body, including body fat percentage and **metabolism**[8]. This led some experts to question whether fitness trackers have really improved on the simpler (and much cheaper) pedometer.

Worse than being a little off, some fitness-tracker features bother health professionals because of what they see as meaningless **metrics**[9]. The sleep tracking modes of some devices, for instance, are attached to the wrist. By recording movement throughout the night, these trackers supposedly measure periods of rest and wakefulness, **quantifying**[10] the amount of restful sleep the user is getting. That would be a very useful feature—if wrist movement were an accurate **indicator** of sleep quality. But sleep researchers point out that brain waves, which the trackers cannot record, are the only good **quantitative** measure of how restful sleep is.

One thing everyone can agree upon is that exercise works. Every little bit counts, and many people do seem to be motivated by **feedback** from the devices. An old saying in management is, "That which is measured improves." So while the difference in value between a $10 pedometer and a $100 fitness tracker may be debatable, either one is better than nothing.

Reading Time: ______ minutes ______ seconds 607 words

4	**fracture**	*n.*	a partial or complete break in a bone
5	**sedentary**	*adj.*	not physically active
6	**counteract**	*v.*	to act against something; to cause something to have less of an effect
7	**point out**	*v.*	to tell someone a fact
8	**metabolism**	*n.*	all the chemical processes in your body, especially the ones that use food
9	**metric**	*n.*	a standard of measurement
10	**quantify**	*v.*	to measure the quantity of

READING COMPREHENSION

A **Mark each statement as true (T) or false (F) according to the reading.**

1. _____ Wearable fitness trackers were becoming popular by 2015.
2. _____ Most fitness trackers include EKG machines.
3. _____ One study showed that counting steps had long-term benefits.
4. _____ Fitness trackers may not be reliable counters of calories burned.
5. _____ One unexpected effect of these devices is more restful sleep.

B **Choose the best answer according to the reading.**

1 What is the main idea of the reading? MAIN IDEA

a. Fitness trackers are popular and seem to motivate people to exercise more.
b. Fitness trackers are a waste of money, and you would be better off with a pedometer.
c. Fitness trackers have some serious problems accurately tracking calories burned.
d. Fitness trackers have developed from simple pedometers with the addition of motion sensors.

2 Which of the following is NOT true of Fitbit? DETAIL

a. James Park is the CEO.
b. The company's IPO was in 2015.
c. Its platform gives users digital "badges."
d. The company's share prices were a result of hype.

3 The word *it* in paragraph 5 refers to ______. REFERENCE

a. device
b. amount
c. accuracy
d. doubt

4 Why do sleep experts criticize the sleep functions of some fitness trackers? DETAIL

a. They are too expensive.
b. They measure the wrong thing.
c. They are no better than pedometers.
d. They fail to measure wrist movement.

C **The following terms are explained in the reading. Write definitions for them.**

1. EKG machine: ______________________________
2. pedometer: ______________________________
3. sedentary lifestyle: ______________________________

SUMMARY

Fill in the blanks with the phrases in the box.

sedentary lifestyles	count steps	track fitness goals
motion sensors	calories burned	brain waves

Definition

- 1 ______________ are an important internal component of fitness trackers.
- The devices record a range of specific variables and help users 2 ______________.

Popularity

- Like pedometers, the trackers 3 ______________, which has proven effective for weight loss.
- People concerned about their 4 ______________ are using fitness trackers at work.

Downsides

- Measurement of 5 ______________ may not be very accurate.
- Sleep specialists criticize sleep features that track wrist movement instead of 6 ______________.

VOCABULARY PRACTICE

Fill in the blanks with the words in the box. Change the form if necessary.

elaborate	feedback	indicator	systematic	pulse	quantitative

1. ______________ measures like test scores may not be the best way to evaluate a student's progress.
2. It is important to not only take ______________ gracefully but to use it in order to improve.
3. A person's IQ is a fairly accurate ______________ of academic and professional potential.
4. If you find someone unconscious, you should immediately check for a(n) ______________.
5. Instead of guessing at your monthly expenditures, find a(n) ______________ way to record them.
6. The couple wants a simple ceremony at home rather than a(n) ______________ and expensive wedding.

SPEAKING

6B Let's Take the Subway

A Model Conversation

Read the conversation. Then listen. Track 37

Kevin: We have a few hours before our flight. Why don't we do some shopping? We haven't spent much time in Union Square yet.

Tori: Well, okay, as long as you're sure we have enough time. We still need to pick up our luggage at the hotel and drop the rental car off.

Kevin: Don't worry; there's plenty of time. I need to get some souvenirs for my family. Otherwise, I know they'll be upset with me. Should we drive?

Tori: No, it's almost **rush hour**. Plus, I heard it's really hard to find parking. What about a streetcar?

Kevin: Too slow. Let's take the BART. Here, I found the map online. We can get on at the station across the street and take the yellow **line** to Powell Street. Then, we can walk to Union Square. We don't even need to **transfer**.

Tori: Great. How much is the **fare**?

Kevin: That **depends on** the distance. The ticket machine will **calculate** that for us.

Tori: All right, let's get going. Unless we leave right now, we'll be **stuck** in a crowded train with all the **commuters**!

Brief note

The Bay Area Rapid Transit or "BART" is a light rail public transportation that operates in San Francisco.

B Vocabulary

Read the conversation again. With a partner, match the bold words in the conversation to the correct definitions.

1. ____________________ in a difficult situation that is hard to get out of
2. ____________________ to find a number using math
3. ____________________ is determined by (something)
4. ____________________ people traveling to or from work
5. ____________________ to change from one bus, train, etc., to another
6. ____________________ the time of day when many people are going to or from work
7. ____________________ a part of a subway or bus system; a certain train or bus route
8. ____________________ the cost of taking a bus, train, etc.

C Vocabulary Comprehension

Look at the map and fill in the blanks in the conversation below. Then listen and check your answers. Track 38

Man: Excuse me. Can I take the subway from the Expo Center to the airport?

Woman: Sure. The ❶ ________________ line goes to Union Station. There, you can ❷ ________________ to the ❸ ________________ line. Then go ❹ ________________ stops to Gateway Station. Transfer to the ❺ ________________ line and go one more stop.

Man: Thanks. What's the ❻ ________________?

Woman: That ❼ ________________ ________________ whether you want a one-way or round-trip ticket.

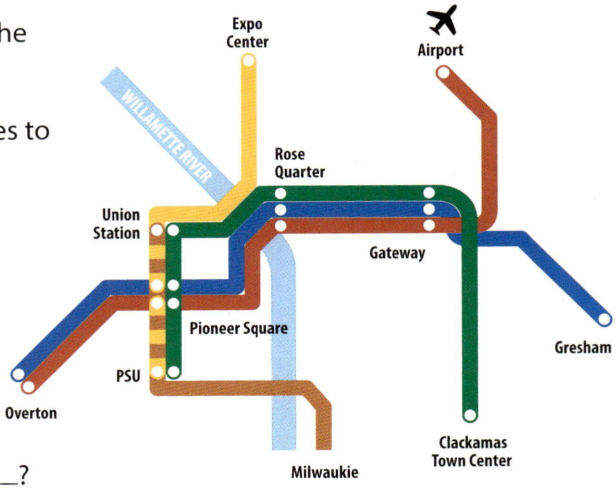

With a partner, practice the conversation. Then take turns choosing two stations on the map and asking your partner for directions from one station to the other.

D Grammar

Ways to express conditions

Brief note

As with other subordinating conjunctions, the two clauses can come in either order.
***As long as** you're sure we have enough time, we can go shopping.*
*We'll be stuck with all the commuters **unless** we leave right now!*

ways to express conditions		
Besides the word *if*, there are several ways to talk about conditions in English.		
expression	**meaning**	**example**
as long as / so long as (conjunctions)	(only) if	We can go shopping **as long as** you're sure we have enough time. (= ... if you're sure we have enough time.)
unless (conjunction)	if not ... then	**Unless** we leave right now, we'll be stuck with all the commuters! (= If we don't leave right now, …)
otherwise (sentence adverb)	if not	I have to get souvenirs for my family. **Otherwise**, they'll be upset. (= ... If not, they'll be upset.)

E Grammar Practice

Fill in the blanks with the correct expressions from the previous page.

1. ____________ we remember to take an umbrella, we should be okay!
2. You should try to leave by four. ____________, you'll get stuck in rush-hour traffic.
3. ____________ the subway is on time, we'll make it to the movie.
4. ____________ you study harder, you won't pass your final exam.
5. You can borrow my car ____________ you return it by midnight.
6. We'll have to cancel the trip ____________ the weather improves.
7. She has to take a taxi, not the bus. ____________, she'll be late.
8. ____________ it all goes smoothly, the show will be a success.

Rewrite the sentences using the given expression.

9. The bus is free if you have a student ID. (as long as)

____

10. If I don't find my keys, I won't be able to give you a ride. (unless)

____

E Use the Language

Subway systems

1. Go online and find a map of a subway, tube, or metro system in another city or country. Describe where it is and give your opinion of it. Does it seem convenient? Does it seem difficult to use? How does it compare to the subway system in your city or country?

2. With a partner, design a subway map for your city or make suggestions to improve your city's subway system. If you could design a whole new subway system to make travel more convenient in your city, what would you do? What would it look like? Draw it and present it to another pair of students. Explain the reasons for your decisions.

WRITING

Divide into teams of two, and choose your topic. Write your argument on the lines below. You will argue in favor of the production and sale of knock-offs, or against it. Present your arguments in front of the class. Each team will have three opportunities to speak. The class will decide whose arguments were most convincing.

Team: ________________________________

Things to Think About

What is wrong with buying knock-offs?
What advantages do people have by buying the knock-offs?
Why are knock-offs cheaper?
How do knock-offs hurt our economy?
How can knock-offs hurt us?
Why do people buy knock-offs?

The production and sale of knock-offs is OK because . . .

1. ________________________________

____

2. ________________________________

____

3. ________________________________

____

The production and sale of knock-offs should be stopped because . . .

1. ________________________________

____

2. ________________________________

____

3. ________________________________

____

SUPPLEMENTAL READING

Exergaming

Track 39

Parents often face a difficult time prying children away from video screens and getting them outdoors for some good old-fashioned exercise. But these parents could actually use kids' love of gaming to get them moving. Exergaming, a combination of physical exercise and video games, makes exercise much more appealing.

A few exergames were released in the 1980s but met with limited success. The first hit exergaming device was Konami's fun and affordable *Dance Dance Revolution*, which came out in 1998. Players stood on a platform and tapped colored arrows with their feet in tune to musical and video cues. Then in the mid-2000s, exergaming really took off. The Nintendo Wii offered players virtual participation in sports like baseball, tennis, and bowling. And CompuTrainer invited riders on a trip through a virtual landscape on a stationary bike—an idea that has had many imitators, including the hugely popular Peloton.

Today, fitness clubs, schools, and community centers in several countries offer exergaming machines. Some schools even include exergaming workouts alongside traditional PE classes. And although parents are happy to see their children exercising, many still worry.

Health experts also have mixed views. "Exergames burn calories, raise heartbeats, and offer a physical benefit for kids," says Lisa Hanson, co-director of a Florida research laboratory. But she adds that it is unclear whether active gaming offers the same benefits as traditional workouts. A recent British study found that many Nintendo Switch fitness games, for example, don't provide intense enough exercise.

Fill in the blanks with information from the reading.

1. The history of exergaming goes all the way back to ______________.
2. The CompuTrainer was a(n) ______________ that takes users through a virtual landscape.
3. Many health experts are not convinced that exergaming has the same benefits as ______________.

EXTENSION Talk or Write About It

Do you or your friends have any exergames? Do you like these types of games? Why or why not?

UNIT 7-1 Finance

Scan for Audio

Pre-Reading Questions

◆ **Think about the following questions.**

1. How do you shop most often, online or in-store? Why?
2. How do you pay for the things you buy? What do you like about that method?
3. Have you always paid that way? Do you think you always will?

VOCABULARY PREVIEW

◆ **Match each word with the correct definition.**

1. click •
2. simplify •
3. resistant •
4. tech •
5. axiom •
6. estimation •

• a. a statement or idea that is generally accepted to be true, but is not necessarily true
• b. not wanting to accept something, especially if it is new
• c. to make something less complicated and easier
• d. a guess or calculation about cost, size, value, etc.
• e. technology; the practical use of scientific discoveries
• f. the act of selecting something on a device by pressing a button

EVOLVING WALLETS

Track 40

"Cash is king" was an **expression**[1] one used to hear quite often. It was meant to suggest that, for customers and **retailers**[2] alike, paper money was the most effective, direct, and powerful means of payment. Over the last twenty years, however, this old axiom might well have been adapted: the card became king. In recent years, contactless card payment has made using a card in-store quicker, more secure, and more **hygienic**[3]. But physical cards remain easy to lose and easy to steal. And, as lifestyles and **consumer**[4] habits continue to change, our wallets are changing, too.

A major factor driving the **payment**[5] revolution is the **growth**[6] of e-commerce. If this was a large market pre-COVID-19, it is now vast. In the past, banks and stores struggled to **keep pace**[7] with online retail. Today, they are left with little choice. They are working with tech companies to improve and simplify methods of payment to keep up with demand.

Q Which types of businesses have found it hard to keep up with e-commerce?

Mobile wallets like ApplePay and GooglePay are perhaps the most widely adopted newer means of payment. These effectively gather all of a customer's bank cards into one smartphone, allowing them to **authorize**[8] payments at the click of a fingerprint-reading button. Other forms of **biometric**[9] authentication, like face and voice recognition, are also improving the security of mobile wallets. The number of smartphone owners increased from 2.5 billion people in 2016 to 3.8 billion in 2021. This makes mobile wallets an increasingly convenient and popular choice.

Q Underline three types of biometric authentication.

1	**expression**	*n.*	a group of words used in a particular situation
2	**retailer**	*n.*	a person, shop, or business that sells things to the public
3	**hygienic**	*adj.*	clean and preventing disease
4	**consumer**	*n.*	a person who buys things for their own use
5	**payment**	*n.*	an amount of money paid, or the act of paying
6	**growth**	*n.*	an increase in the size or importance of something

What effect has e-commerce had on shoppers' attitudes when in-store?

a. They feel pleased to see goods in person.
b. They feel frustrated by how long it takes.

Stores are also trying to ensure a more convenient experience for customers. Mobile Point of Sale (POS) technology gives customers the ability to pay anywhere within a store or even at a market stall. By carrying a small wireless device, staff effectively bring the register to the customer. This is a real advantage because the convenience of e-commerce has left many customers too impatient to wait in slow-moving lines.

Avoiding close contact while shopping is also going to be a priority. That's why some stores are making use of biometric authentication themselves. Customers at Amazon Go stores in the US need not even reach for their smartphones. They pay simply by **scanning**[10] their hands. Amazon is clearly ahead of the times, but it plans to bring its technology to other stores soon.

Not everyone is convinced, however. Some shoppers may be **resistant** to handing over personal information like hand-prints to large corporations. They worry about how this data could be used. Also, for some older people, or those without the money to purchase new technology, the pace of change may be too fast. The form money takes will almost certainly continue evolving. Even those who feel up-to-date may soon find themselves behind the times. Wallets, whether leather or mobile, may be living on borrowed time.

Reading Time: _______ minutes _______ seconds 457 words

7	**keep pace**	*v.*	to go or make progress at the same speed as (someone or something else)
8	**authorize**	*v.*	to give formal permission for something to happen
9	**biometric**	*adj.*	using a person's characteristics, e.g., their voice or the pattern of their eyes, to prove who they are
10	**scan**	*v.*	to use a piece of technology to get information from something such as a bank card or a part of the body

READING COMPREHENSION

A **Mark each statement as true (T) or false (F) according to the reading.**

1. _____ Until recent decades, cash was the main way people paid for things.
2. _____ The popularity of mobile wallets is linked to the popularity of smartphones.
3. _____ Mobile Point of Sale technology allows people to shop from home.
4. _____ Smartphones are an important part of Amazon Go's payment system.
5. _____ Factors like income and age could leave some people behind.

B **Choose the best answer according to the reading.**

1 What is the main idea of the reading? MAIN IDEA

a. E-commerce is forcing stores to adapt.
b. The way people pay for things is changing.
c. New technologies cause people to spend more.
d. Cash will soon no longer exist.

2 In paragraph 1, the word *effective* is closest in meaning to _________. VOCABULARY

a. affordable
b. functional
c. seasonal
d. typical

3 Which of the following is different from others? DETAIL

a. ApplePay
b. Cash
c. Amazon Go
d. GooglePay

4 What can be inferred from paragraph 5? INFERENCE

a. Technology is very popular with staff in stores.
b. Stores can save paper by using technology.
c. Customers do not trust technology in stores yet.
d. Shoppers can be kept safer by technology in stores.

C **Look for the answers in the reading and write them on the lines.**

1. How do staff in stores make use of mobile POS technology?

____

2. Why might some customers not want to use Amazon Go stores?

____

SUMMARY

Fill in the blanks with the phrases in the box.

estimated to be	means of payment	quick and secure
mobile POS technology	face recognition	contactless way

Past

- Cash was seen as the most practical 1 ______________________ for many years.
- Later, cards became popular and were the first 2 ______________________ of paying.

Present

- E-commerce is 3 ______________________ worth around $5 trillion.
- Customers use mobile wallets because they are a(n) 4 ______________________ way of paying for things anywhere.
- In stores, 5 ______________________ is helping to make buying things easier.

Future

- Businesses want to find more contactless ways of paying.
- 6 ______________________ and other forms of biometric authentication will mean we won't need any equipment to pay for things.

VOCABULARY PRACTICE

Fill in the blanks with the words in the box. Change the form if necessary.

resistant	simplify	click	tech	axiom

1. Applying for a visa is too complicated. The process should be ____________________.
2. Luis is good with computers and plans to have a career in ____________________.
3. Our company believes in the ____________________ that the customer is always right.
4. Online news sites use shocking headlines to get more ____________________.
5. Teenagers can often be very ____________________ when their parents ask them to do chores.

SPEAKING

7A Spending Habits

A Warm-up

Talk about the questions as a class.

1. What do you enjoy about shopping?
2. Are there some things you enjoy shopping for more than others?

B Multi-Text

1. Read the texts. Then answer the questions.

Text 1

Income and Spending in the United States, 2015-2016

	2015	2016	% change
Average income before taxes	**$69,629**	**$74,664**	**7.2%**
Average annual spending	**$55,978**	**$57,311**	**2.4%**
Food	$7,023	$7,203	2.6%
Housing	$18,409	$18,806	2.6%
Clothes	$1,846	$1,803	-2.3%
Transportation	$9,503	$9,409	-4.8%
Healthcare	$4,342	$4,612	6.2%
Entertainment	$2,842	$2,913	2.5%
Insurance	$6,349	$6,831	7.6%
Other	$3,845	$3,933	2.3%

Talk about

1. What were Americans' three biggest expenses in 2015-2016? Do you think that these expenses are similar in most countries?
2. Do you ever have the problem described by BigSpender?
3. What rule does Shopaholic have for shopping? Do you have any shopping rules for yourself?

Brief note

An impulse is a sudden feeling. An *impulse buy* is a purchase that you make without planning or thinking about it first.

Text 2

BigSpender 2 hours ago

I love going into stores and seeing all the latest fashions, gadgets, and accessories. I also love hunting for a bargain. But my shopping behavior makes it difficult to properly plan my expenses. I always pay my bills and rent, of course. But sometimes, when I'm bored or in a bad mood, I'll go shopping and use my credit card on impulse buys. This wasn't so bad when I was younger. I had plenty of money and fewer bills. But now I have to think about the future. My goal right now is saving up for a wedding and buying a house. My girlfriend and I are planning to get married next year. After that, I have to think about saving for our future children! It feels like a big change in my life. Do any of you have tips on how I can control my shopping habits?

Text 3

Brief note

The phrase *go ahead* is often used to give permission or encouragement to do something.

Comments:

Shopaholic **23 minutes ago**

You said that you love hunting for a bargain. Do you shop online or in stores?

> **BigSpender** **19 minutes ago**
>
> I do all my shopping in stores. There's a big department store by my office, where I usually go for lunch and dinner.

Shopaholic **15 minutes ago**

You should definitely stop shopping on your lunch break. You said yourself that you're an impulse buyer. So don't give yourself the opportunity. If you enjoy looking for bargains, go online instead. The prices are often lower on the Internet. Also, since you can't see the products in person, you will be less likely to buy things you don't need. Here's a tip—and this is a rule that I've made for myself: If you're about to buy something in a store, stop. If you're still thinking about the item three days later, then go ahead and get it!

2. Decide which text each question refers to. Choose 1, 2, or 3, and write it on the lines.

Which text...

says that shopping online is cheaper? ________

explains a shopping problem? ________

mentions how feelings can cause more spending? ________

includes information on many people's spending habits? ________

3. Complete the following statements with exact information from the texts.

1. Average annual spending in the US increased by ____________ from 2015 to 2016.
2. BigSpender likes to shop for electronics, clothes, and ____________.
3. According to Shopaholic, you should wait for ____________ before spending money on something.
4. BigSpender wants to save money for his ____________ and a(n) ____________.
5. From 2015 to 2016, Americans' spending on ____________ increased the most.

C Vocabulary

1. Circle the word that is closest in meaning to the word in bold.

1. **properly**	clearly	correctly	often	cheaply
2. **income**	budget	item	pay	savings
3. **annual**	frequent	usual	rare	yearly
4. **opportunity**	chance	sale	decision	advice
5. **behavior**	rules	plans	ideas	actions

2. Fill in the blanks with the correct words from the box.

bargain	wedding	average	tax	healthcare

1. The price is $4.50, but with ________________ the total will be $4.95.
2. Since they're inviting 150 people to the ________________, it will be quite expensive.
3. Older people get sick more often, so they have to spend more money on ________________.
4. I found a used TV online for just $70—what a(n) ________________!
5. The ________________ person spends more on housing than on anything else.

D In Your World

What do you enjoy buying?

Discuss the following questions with a partner.

1. On average, what do you spend the most money on each month?
2. Look at Text 3 in activity B again. Do you think that Shopaholic is right about shopping online? What do you buy online?
3. Do you have any other advice for BigSpender? Do you have any shopping behavior that you'd like to change?

WRITING

Interview another student about their thoughts or opinions regarding the topic of commercial holidays. Three questions have been provided for you. You must also think of TWO additional questions. Record your partner's answers on the lines below, and then report back to the class using complete sentences.

Partner: ______________________________

1. What do you think about companies creating their own special days to promote their products?

____

____

____

2. Do you think it is fair that companies take advantage of their customers' emotions and put pressure on them to buy their products on certain days? Why or why not?

____

____

____

3. What are some enjoyable things about commercial holidays? Give examples.

____

____

____

4. (Student Question) ______________________________

____

____

____

5. (Student Question) ______________________________

____

____

____

SUPPLEMENTAL READING

The Developing Digital Economy

Track 41

The COVID-19 pandemic sank the world into a recession which caused the global economy to shrink by 4.3 percent in the first year alone. However, with stores closed and people mostly staying home, some e-commerce businesses saw their profits and stock prices rise sharply. Before the pandemic, Amazon, for example, was valued at $920 billion. One year later, it was worth $1.49 trillion.

Some other e-commerce businesses also made more money due to the virus outbreak. Mercado Libre provides similar services to Amazon in eighteen South American countries. Its business doubled during the pandemic. However, very few companies gained financially from the virus, and those that did were mostly based in the US or China.

Obviously, the benefits of the digital economy are not open to everyone. Already at an economic disadvantage, many developing nations run the risk of being left further behind. In those countries, face-to-face deals often remain the best, most secure way to shop, and cash is still the primary means of payment. Across Africa, for example, it is estimated that only twenty-two percent of people have access to the Internet.

Dr. Amani Abou-Zeid is responsible for increasing access to the digital economy in the African Union. She leads the African Digital Transformation Strategy (ADTS). By installing a vast network of broadband cables across the continent, the ADTS plans to bring 300 million more African citizens online by 2025. Abou-Zeid hopes that African and international e-commerce businesses will pay for most of these developments. In her view, it is these companies that will benefit most in the long run. This is something Amazon's success would seem to confirm.

Fill in the blanks with information from the reading.

1. Some ______________________ companies made large profits during the COVID-19 pandemic.
2. In developing countries, people often pay with ______________________.
3. Dr. Amani Abou-Zeid has a plan to install ______________________ across Africa.

EXTENSION Talk or Write About It

Overall, do you think the digital economy is a good thing? Why or why not? How do you think we will pay for things in the future? How do you feel about that?

UNIT 7-2 Finance

Scan for Audio

Pre-Reading Questions

◆ **Think about the following questions.**

1. Can you think of any examples of crowdfunding?
2. If you were going to participate in crowdfunding, what kind of business or organization would you like to invest in?
3. What do you think might be the advantages of crowdfunding for individuals and businesses?

VOCABULARY PREVIEW

◆ **Match each word with the correct definition.**

1. trajectory •	• a. collection of investments that are owned by a particular person or organization
2. distribution •	• b. done without much planning because of a sudden feeling or impulse
3. virtue •	• c. the right of people or groups to have a similar position and receive the same treatment
4. portfolio •	• d. an advantage or benefit
5. equality •	• e. the way in which people or things are spread out
6. spontaneous •	• f. a process of change or development that leads toward a particular result

HOW DEMOCRATIC IS CROWDFUNDING?

Track 42

The basic concept behind crowdfunding is simple: a relatively large number of investors contribute a small amount each to finance a project, business, or organization. There are two main ways in which this could be seen as democratic. First, it can give individual investors a strong sense of involvement in the way companies and projects are run. Second, it is often said to give smaller, newer companies a chance to compete against larger, established ones.

Crowdfunding is not a new idea. As far back as 1700, a large group of investors provided loans for poor families in Ireland. Nearly 300 years later, in 1997, the first instance of modern crowdfunding is said to have occurred when British rock group Marillion financed a US tour by asking fans for donations. This was possible because many fans of the band were **early adopters**[1] of the Internet. Today, with the rest of the world joining them online, organizations and businesses have a worldwide pool of investors to draw upon.

Q Why was the band Marillion able to use crowdfunding?

In the years after 1997, much crowdfunding remained **focused on**[2] artistic projects, charities, and not-for-profit organizations; this is usually based on reward crowdfunding (RCF). RCF does not promise investors any financial return. Instead, those who donate might, for example, be mentioned by name in the book, film, or building that they help to fund. RCF is now also being used by entrepreneurs as well—they promise **participants**[3] a product or service in return for their money should the business succeed. With fairly low rewards, business-based RCF investments are usually small, too, at an average of just $99 in 2020.

Another way of generating investment is equity crowdfunding (ECF), which is mostly used by businesses. Like stocks and shares, this promises investors a financial return. Through accessible websites like Crowdcube, Fundable, and IndieGoGo, ordinary people invest small amounts at relatively low risk. ECF is particularly helpful to **start-ups**[4] and small and medium-sized **enterprises**[5] (SMEs). The financial crash in 2008 left banks nervous about giving loans to start-ups and SMEs, so, needing an alternative, many businesses turned to ECF for its greater **equality** of

Q Underline three places where those interested in crowdfunding could look.

1	**early adopter**	*n.*	someone who is one of the first people to start using a new product, especially a new piece of technology
2	**focus on**	*v.*	to give a lot of attention to one particular person, subject, or thing
3	**participant**	*n.*	a person who takes part in or becomes involved in a particular activity
4	**start-up**	*n.*	a small business that has recently started
5	**enterprise**	*n.*	an organization, especially a business

opportunity. By June 2017, in the UK alone, 400,000 investors had put some $700 million into 1,538 different business ideas.

As well as providing much-needed investment, ECF has several other **virtues**. It allows start-ups and SMEs to develop at their own pace. Without the pressure caused by being in debt to banks, businesses can take more risks and innovate. Another advantage is that the individuals who invest in ECF are more likely to **engage with**[6] the business than traditional shareholders, offering feedback and suggestions along the way. This is good for the company's development, and investors—whatever they contribute—feel they have an influence on the **trajectory** of the business.

However, crowdfunding may not be quite as democratic as it first appears; although money is spread between more companies, investors still invest in some more than others. The clue is in the name: in crowdfunding, people often follow the crowd. So, while new entrepreneurs can benefit from ECF and RCF, investors are often most attracted to those with a track record of success; even with small investments, individuals tend to be cautious. Also, businesses with more initial funds can afford more publicity and can **pursue**[7] more potential investors. The **geographical**[8] **distribution** of successful businesses is not equal either. Those in certain areas—often around university campuses—tend to do far better.

Crowdfunding is never totally risk-free, and between 2011 and 2015, eighteen percent of all crowdfunded businesses in the UK failed completely, leaving individuals with little or nothing to show for their money. Over the same period of time, of crowdfunded businesses supported by "experts," none failed. This would suggest that thorough research is essential, but amateur investors tend to be quite **spontaneous**. According to one study, on average, crowdfunders do just twenty minutes of research **prior to**[9] investing. Those with training and specialist knowledge, on the other hand, are far more likely to see significant gains from ECF investments. So, rather than remaining a way for ordinary people to invest small amounts, ECF is becoming a way for venture capitalists—experts in risky investments—to expand their **portfolios** and make large amounts of profit; investment groups and even banks are increasingly investing in ECF, too.

Crowdfunding undoubtedly has the potential to be a dynamic, democratic way for artists, start-ups, and SMEs to generate funds. It also allows smaller investors to feel engaged and involved. However, it may also prove to be a victim of its own success as professional investors increasingly dominate the crowdfunding landscape.

Reading Time: ______ minutes ______ seconds 764 words

[6] **engage with** *v.* to become involved, or have contact, with someone or something
[7] **pursue** *v.* to go after a person or group in order to persuade them to do something
[8] **geographical** *adj.* relating to geography, where things are, or to a particular place
[9] **prior to** *adv.* existing or happening before something else, or before a particular time

READING COMPREHENSION

A **Mark each statement as true (T) or false (F) according to the reading.**

1. _____ Less-wealthy people in Ireland benefited from crowdfunding.
2. _____ RCF mainly suits organizations whose priority is making money.
3. _____ Thanks to the financial crash, banks were not keen to lend money to smaller businesses.
4. _____ Businesses funded by ECF have freedom to try new things.
5. _____ A typical ECF investor carefully studies a company before making a contribution.

B **Choose the best answer according to the reading.**

1. What is the main topic of the reading? TOPIC
   a. The ways crowdfunding is helping charities to grow
   b. The different methods for businesses to raise funds
   c. The biggest crowdfunding success stories
   d. The advantages and disadvantages of crowdfunding
2. In paragraph 2, the word *them* refers to _____. REFERENCE
   a. donations
   b. fans
   c. organizations
   d. investors
3. What is the purpose of paragraph 6? PURPOSE
   a. To urge potential crowdfunders to be cautious before investing
   b. To explain reasons why crowdfunding investments are unequal
   c. To discuss what companies can do to attract more investors
   d. To clarify the psychology of risks and rewards in crowdfunding
4. Which group of people has the highest chance of making money? DETAIL
   a. Venture capitalists
   b. RCF investors
   c. University students
   d. Amateur investors

C **Fill in the blanks with information from the reading.**

1. Organizations and business are able to draw upon a worldwide _____________________ online.
2. ECF differs from RCF in that it offers investors a(n) _____________________.
3. Amateur investors tend to be quite _____________________, meaning they do not do much research before making investments.

SUMMARY

An introductory sentence for a brief summary of the passage is given below. Choose three more sentences to complete the summary.

First Sentence: While it seems democratic, crowdfunding may give more advantages to some than others.

1. By 2017, 400,000 people in the UK had invested in crowdfunding.
2. Ordinary people often do not have sufficient knowledge to invest in the best businesses.
3. The financial crash meant that banks stopped lending money to SMEs.
4. Businesses near universities often attract high levels of investment.
5. Business people with a long record of success usually appeal to investors more than those run by graduates.
6. The financial crash meant banks were nervous about giving loans to start-ups and SMEs.

VOCABULARY PRACTICE

Fill in the blanks with the words in the box. Change the form if necessary.

virtue	equality	distribution	trajectory	portfolio	spontaneous

1. Although developed countries are wealthy, the ________________ of this wealth among the population is rarely equal.
2. Since the COVID-19 pandemic began, home shopping platforms have seen their profits remain on an upward ________________.
3. In the early 20th century, a group of women known as suffragettes fought for ________________, including the right to vote.
4. Experts recommend that shareholders keep a diverse ________________ of investments as it is less risky.
5. The ________________ of solar energy include its cost, sustainability, and the fact it reduces the burning of fossil fuels.
6. Dr. Harrow follows a strict daily routine and rarely does anything ________________.

SPEAKING

7B Credit Cards

A Vocabulary

Look up the pronunciation and meaning of these words. Then listen. Track 43

interest

account

balance

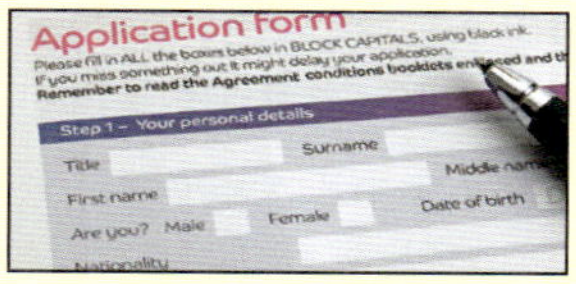

application

due date

transaction

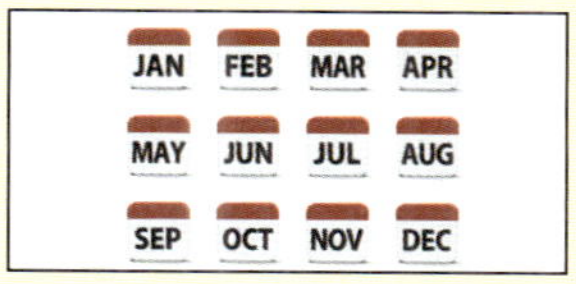

monthly

payment

B Authentic Text

1. Read the credit card information and application.

Bank Today Silver Card

Application

FEES	
Annual Membership Fee	$0 fee for the first year; $75 every year after that
Transaction Fees	
Balance Transfer Fee	5% of the amount transferred; $5 minimum
Foreign Transaction Fee	None
Late Payment Fees	$15 if the balance is less than $100 $27 if the balance is between $100 and $300 $37 if the balance is more than $300

INTEREST CHARGES	
How to avoid paying interest on purchases	The due date will be 21 days after the date on your bill. You will not be charged interest on purchases if you pay your balance by the due date each month.
Minimum Interest Charge	None

First name	Middle initial	Surname	
Daniel	L.	Munroe	
Mailing address 1		**Mailing address 2**	
335 19th St.		Apt. 201	
City		**State**	**ZIP code**
Springfield		IA	50001

Check the types of accounts you own.	Checking	Savings
	✓	
Type of home	**Monthly housing payment**	
Apartment	$750.00	
Annual income		
$ 38,000.00		
Employer		
Worldwide Insurance, Inc.		

2. Read the email and fill in the blanks with the correct words from the box.

interest	minimum	avoid	membership	fees	account	monthly	transactions

Dear Mr. Munroe,

Your recent application for a Bank Today Silver Card has been accepted. Congratulations on your ❶ ______________! Your card will arrive at your mailing address within five business days. When you receive it, please call 1-888-9067 to confirm that you have your card and to activate it. Then you can begin making ❷ ______________.

You will receive a(n) ❸ ______________ bill in the mail. Each bill will state your current balance as well as the ❹ ______________ required payment for the preceding month. You can pay by check or online. With either option, we must receive at least the minimum payment on or before the due date. In this way, you can ❺ ______________ paying late ❻ ______________. But remember that if you pay your whole balance every month, you will not have to pay ❼ ______________ on your transactions.

If you have any questions, please contact us. You can also manage your ❽ ______________ online at BankToday.com.

Sincerely,
Bank Today Customer Service

C Grammar

Each, every, either, neither

Brief note

Each, *either*, and *neither* can also be used alone as pronouns: *Each receives a bill. Either is fine. Neither charges an annual fee.*

each, every, either, neither			
The words *each*, *every*, *either*, and *neither* can come before singular countable nouns. *Each*, *either*, and *neither* can also come before pronouns, but must be followed by *of*. Before plural nouns, they must be followed by *of* + determiner.			
	meaning	**before a singular noun**	**before a plural noun / pronoun**
each	all the members of a group (focus on the individual)	I receive a bill **each** month.	**Each of their** customers receives a bill. **Each of** them receives a bill.
every	all the members of a group (focus on the group)	It's good to pay your bills **every** month.	
either	of two options: A or B	**Either** option for payment is fine.	**Either of the** options is fine. **Either of** them is fine.
neither	of two options: not A and not B	**Neither** bank charges an annual fee.	**Neither of the** banks charges an annual fee. **Neither of** them charges an annual fee.

Circle the correct words.

1. It's a good idea to have a different password for every (account / accounts) that you have.
2. I'm careful about (each / every) of my credit card purchases.
3. You can have fun shopping at either (the / of the) two department stores in town.
4. We accept all credit cards at this store, so you can use (either / neither) of those.

D Use the Language

Comparing Cards

Work with a partner. If you had to choose either of the credit cards below, which one would you choose? Explain your choice to the class.

	Mobile Bank Card	Shine Freedom Card
Interest	No interest for first 12 months; 10% after that	No interest for first 18 months; 18% after that
Annual fee	$80	None
Special offers	5% discount at most supermarkets	7% discount at popular restaurants and cafés

MEMO

WRITING

1. What do you do when you have extra money? Do you spend it or save it?

2. Where do you want to spend your money when you get a job in the future?

SUPPLEMENTAL READING

Veronica Mars: A Crowdfunding Success Story?

Track 44

In 2004, a new drama appeared on the US channel United Paramount Network. Aimed at teenagers and young adults, *Veronica Mars* told the story of a young woman who was in the process of graduating high school and moving on to college while also working as a private investigator.

The first season was a hit, regularly attracting 2.5 million viewers and winning several awards. But in 2007, after four seasons, the show was canceled, and shocked fans were told it would not return. The show's writer, Rob Thomas, announced he was working on a movie version, but his idea was declined by major studios. For many movies, this would have been the end of the story, but a friend had told Thomas about a relatively new website.

Kickstarter is a crowdfunding site that focuses on finding backers for creative projects, and in 2013, Thomas used it to announce that he was looking to raise $2 million to make the *Veronica Mars* movie. Those donating $10 would be emailed a PDF of the movie's script upon its release. Larger donations would bring rewards, including stickers, T-shirts, signed posters, and personal messages from cast members. Those donating $5,000 would be given a private screening of the movie before its release.

Thanks to social media, news of the project spread quickly, and the target of $2 million was reached in just eleven hours. By the end of the fundraising drive, 91,585 backers—still more than any other project in the history of Kickstarter—had given a total of $5,702,153. The film was finally released in 2014 and, though popular with fans, made only $3.5 million back in ticket sales. One certain winner was Kickstarter, though, as the website receives five percent of the money every project raises.

Fill in the blanks with information from the reading.

1. The show was ____________________ young audiences.
2. After his film was turned down, Rob Thomas was told about ____________________ by a friend.
3. The film raised more on Kickstarter than it made in ____________________.

EXTENSION Talk or Write About It

What do you think is good about crowdfunding? How do you think it can help individuals and organizations? Who might it not help so much?

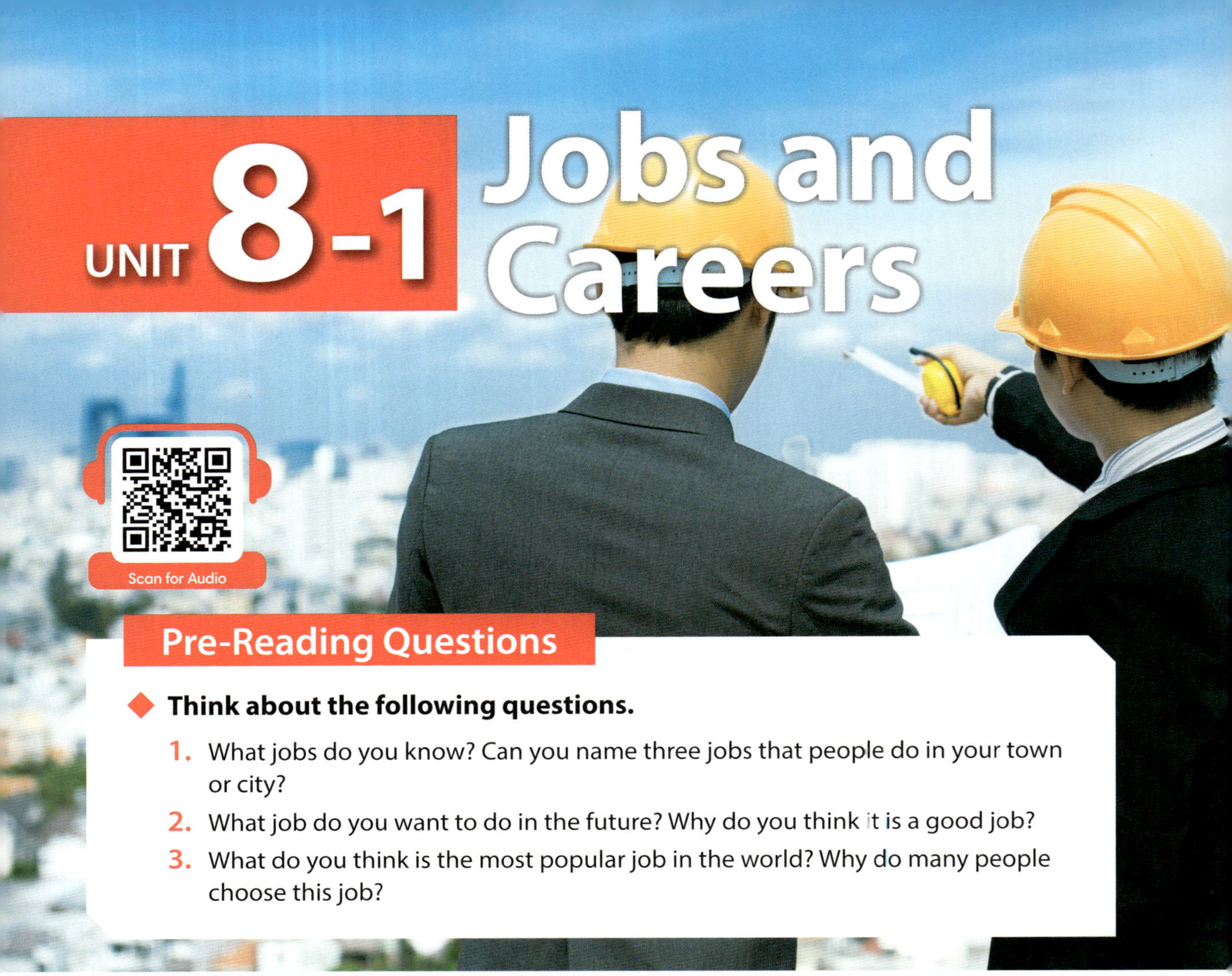

UNIT 8-1 Jobs and Careers

Scan for Audio

Pre-Reading Questions

◆ **Think about the following questions.**

1. What jobs do you know? Can you name three jobs that people do in your town or city?
2. What job do you want to do in the future? Why do you think it is a good job?
3. What do you think is the most popular job in the world? Why do many people choose this job?

VOCABULARY PREVIEW

◆ **Read the definitions. Then match each word in bold with its definition.**

A. money available to a business or person
B. old; past middle age
C. special care or treatment
D. of or relating to cities and the people who live in them
E. a person who studies something closely to get information from it

1. ___________ Many people are moving from rural areas to **urban** ones.
2. ___________ Most businesses need accountants to handle their **finances**.
3. ___________ Some people need a lot of **medical attention** when they get older.
4. ___________ The position of a systems **analyst** is highly valued in some companies.
5. ___________ The world's population is starting to include more and more **elderly** people.

What Will You Do When You Graduate?

Track 45

In college, many students choose a career that will last a lifetime. The thought of finding the right job when they graduate makes some students anxious. The good news for those who are unsure is that a number of jobs will see growth in the future.

Business experts believe that health care will be the best industry for employment. Over half of the world's population will reach old age in the coming years. The elderly require a lot of medical attention. Nurses and physician assistants are both important to health care institutions, and these jobs should see the most growth. In fact, the field of nursing is expected to grow by twenty-three percent.

▲ Yearly salaries of select jobs (in US dollars)

The number of physician assistants will increase by about forty percent.

Another industry that will boom over the next twenty years is the computer industry. Programmers will continue to be in demand. Those with practical experience will be even more valuable to large companies. There is an expected thirty-four percent increase in the number of programmers. The position of systems analyst is also highly valued, and that field should grow by twenty percent.

Other growing areas may not seem as exciting. Civil engineering involves planning transportation and development in urban areas. Urban planning will become even more important as people continue to move from rural areas into urban areas. So civil engineering will grow by about twenty-four percent. Likewise, accounting will remain important. There are few businesses that do not need an accountant to handle their finances. The position is likely to see a twenty-two percent increase in the future.

In an ever-changing job market, many types of jobs are expected to see growth in the future. Selecting from one of the fields that is expected to grow will help you make a decision when it is time to choose a career that is right for you!

Reading Time: _______ minutes _______ seconds 310 words

Review the Highlights

◆ **Mark up the text and infographic according to the instructions.**

1. Look at Paragraph 2. Circle the industry that experts believe will need the most workers in the future.
2. Look at Paragraph 2. Circle who will need a lot of medical attention.
3. Look at Paragraph 3. Underline who will be valuable in the computer industry.
4. Look at Paragraph 4. Put a star next to the job that involves development of urban areas.
5. Look at the infographic. Write the job that makes the highest salary of all. ___________
6. Look at the infographic. Write the job that makes the lowest salary of all. ___________

READING COMPREHENSION

A **Circle the correct answer.**

1. What is the good news for students who graduate? Details: what
   a. There will be more jobs in rural areas.
   b. A number of jobs will see growth.
   c. The world's population will be older.
   d. Programmers will not be in demand.

2. Which field will see the most growth in the future? Details: which
   a. Civil engineering
   b. Accounting
   c. Health care
   d. Computer programming

3. What do companies in the computer industry value? Details: what
   a. Practical experience
   b. Systems analysts
   c. Engineers
   d. The elderly

4. What is NOT true about civil engineering? Negative fact
   a. It will grow by twenty-four percent.
   b. It involves transportation.
   c. It is needed in urban planning.
   d. It is part of the health care industry.

5. What is the purpose of the reading? Purpose
   a. To persuade graduates to go into health care
   b. To help students choose a job for the future
   c. To assist large finance companies
   d. To help students graduate

B **Complete the summary. Write the words from the reading that best fit in the blanks. One word is extra.**

urban graduate engineering attention finances elderly physician analysts

Many college students are worried about what career path to take once they 1. _______________. The good news is that a number of fields will see growth in the future. 2. _______________ assistant and nursing positions will both see growth. Jobs in the health care industry are generally a good choice because 3. _______________ people make up a large percentage of the world's population, and they need a lot of medical 4. _______________. The computer industry will also grow. Programmers and systems 5. _______________ will be needed. Civil 6. _______________ jobs will also be in demand. These positions involve transportation and 7. _______________ planning. Although the job market is always changing, there are many career possibilities for college graduates.

SUMMARY

1. Read the job descriptions listed below. Can you add anything to them?

Teacher – helps others learn; ______

Artist – makes art with paint, clay, sculpture, or photography; ______

Baker – bakes cakes, cookies, bread, etc.; ______

Lawyer – helps explain the law to others; ______

Astronomer – studies the stars and space; ______

Architect – designs buildings or houses; ______

Farmer – plants food to grow and sell; ______

Gardener – grows and cares for plants; ______

Dentist – fixes medical problems in people's mouths; ______

2. Once you have finalized the descriptions, discuss the jobs with your partner. Make sure to answer the questions below as you talk.

What kind of training is required to perform each job?
Which jobs would you want to do? Why?
Which jobs would you not want to do? Why?

3. Choose one of the topics below and discuss it with your partner.

1. Why did you choose the major you chose?
2. What would you like to do when you graduate? What is your dream job?

VOCABULARY PRACTICE

Fill in the blanks with the words in the box. Change the form if necessary.

unsure	reach	boom	remain	civil

1. We finally ______ Daegu after 4 hours of driving.
2. I was ______ about how many people will come to the party.
3. Many Korean undergraduate students want to be a ______ servant because of job stability.
4. Please ______ seated.
5. There was a baby ______ in Korea after the Korean War.

SPEAKING

8A What's a Social Media Manager?

A Warm-up

Talk about the question as a class.

Have you ever communicated with a company on social media?

B Authentic Text

1. **Read and listen to the online article. Then answer the questions.** Track 46

Brief note

To be *on call* means that "although you are not at work, you may be called at any time if you are needed."

Social Media Managers: FAQ

by Alec Rodriguez

I'm a social media manager for a chain of clothing stores. Since this job is a fairly new one, people often ask me about it. Here are answers to some of the most frequently asked questions.

Q: What do social media managers do?

A: I manage my company's online communications. I'm responsible for our Facebook page, X and Instagram accounts, and our other social media sites. Every day, I post messages, photos, and videos to create a positive impression of our brand. In addition, I analyze data about which content is most popular. I also monitor and respond to customers' comments, and I research our competitors' social media accounts. Social media managers are important because one study found that almost 75 percent of consumers are more likely to buy from a company that is active on social media.

Q: What are the qualifications?

A: You must have lots of experience with social media and be willing to work outside of the usual business hours. The Internet doesn't close at 5 p.m. every day! You're on call twenty-four hours a day, seven days a week. You must also have strong writing skills. Another qualification is to know your audience. For example, my company specializes in clothes for people in their teens and twenties. To do my job well, I need to understand the tastes and attitudes of young people, and keep up with the latest trends. There's one more qualification I should mention: a thick skin! As everyone knows, people aren't always very nice online. You must be able to respond to complaints and even insults calmly.

Q: Is it hard to get a job as a social media manager?

A: Yes, it's a very competitive field. To get a job as a social media manager, you must show companies that you are passionate about things using your own personal social media activity. And you should start now! Be active on several different sites, and create a blog. Make sure your posts are unique, intelligent, and funny. And don't forget to be polite. If you have an unpleasant personality online, potential employers will find out, and it'll hurt your chances of getting a good job.

Brief note

People with a *thick skin* (thick-skinned people) are not easily upset or hurt if they are criticized. In contrast, people who have a thin skin (thin-skinned people) are easily upset or hurt by criticism.

2. Talk about the questions after you read and listen.

1. How important do you think social media managers are for a company's success?
2. The writer says that "people aren't always very nice online." What do you think he means? Can you give any examples?
3. Do you think employers should be allowed to look at people's private social media accounts?

3. Identify the main purpose of this article.

a. to persuade people to become social media managers

b. to provide basic information about being a social media manager

c. to describe the writer's experiences as a social media manager

4. Choose the correct answers.

1. Which is NOT part of the writer's job?
   a. replying to customers
   b. looking at data
   c. making sales
   d. putting content online
2. Why does the writer mention a study?
   a. to show that companies benefit from social media managers
   b. to show that social media is becoming more popular
   c. to show that he has a thick skin
   d. to show that he analyzes content
3. What is implied about the writer?
   a. He seldom works at night.
   b. He makes a high salary.
   c. He majored in English.
   d. He knows about fashion.
4. What does the writer state about the company that he works for?
   a. It is new.
   b. It has young customers.
   c. It sells mobile devices.
   d. It is currently hiring.
5. What does the writer advise readers to do?
   a. be pleasant online
   b. apply to many companies
   c. complain about online rudeness
   d. avoid addiction to social media

C Vocabulary

1. Write the words from the box under the correct pictures.

consumer	unique	data	insult	monitor

1. ______________ **2.** ______________ **3.** ______________ **4.** ______________ **5.** ______________

2. Match the words with the correct definitions.

1. specialize •　　• a. a person, team, or company that is competing with others

2. respond •　　• b. to spend most of your time doing one type of work or studying one subject

3. analyze •　　• c. possible

4. potential •　　• d. to examine the details of (something) carefully in order to understand it

5. competitor •　　• e. to say or write something as an answer; to reply

D In Your World

Social Media Managers

Discuss the questions with a partner.

1. Do you think you would enjoy being a social media manager? Would you be good at it? Why or why not?

2. Go online and research the social media activity of two companies or brands that you are interested in. Did you learn anything new about them? Do they make a good impression? Share your opinions with the class.

WRITING

1. Have you had a part-time job? If not, where would you like to work part-time?

2. Would you like to work in a foreign country? Why or why not?

SUPPLEMENTAL READING

Keimyung Caritas

Track 47

Caritas means love, virtue, and charity. It is the Latin translation of the Greek word "Agape," which in English is translated into "Charity." Originally, Caritas referred to God's love for humanity as revealed through the cross of Jesus Christ, and in response, the love that humans show towards God and their neighbors. Today, Keimyung Caritas is the name of the coalition of the "Keimyung 1% Sharing Love," a non-profit organization established within Keimyung University, Dongsan Medical Center, and Keimyung College University.

In 2004, Keimyung University launched the Keimyung 1% Sharing Love initiative to commemorate the 50th anniversary of its undergraduate education institution. The predecessor of this movement was the "Hospital Evangelization Society," founded in 1921, which later evolved into the "Dongsan Medical Mission and Welfare Society," a non-profit corporation. The society's members used to donate 1% of their salary to support overseas medical missionary work. To put the spirit of sharing into practice, Keimyung University operates the 1% Sharing Love initiative, where faculty and staff donate 1% of their salaries to create funds that support volunteer work for disadvantaged communities and underdeveloped regions lagging behind in global progress. These funds are used to provide relief in various forms, such as medical care, education, and environmental assistance, to places in urgent need.

Notably, Keimyung University has also provided scholarships to outstanding students from developing countries. By supporting them, the university practices its founding principles and fosters talented individuals who will play key roles in forming diplomatic relationships with their home countries. Each year, up to 10 students from Asia, Africa, South America, and Eastern Europe are selected. These students receive benefits such as full tuition coverage for the entire duration of their studies, including one year of Korean language training, dormitory expenses, and living stipends.

Source: 빛을 여는 계명인. 계명대학교 출판부. 2024. p.199–205.

EXTENSION Talk or Write About It

1. What charities do you know about? What do they do?
2. Have you ever donated to a charity? If so, which one?
3. If you created a non-profit organization, what kind of work would it do?

UNIT 8-2 Jobs and Careers

Scan for Audio

Pre-Reading Questions

◆ **Think about the following questions.**

1. Are most companies controlled by men or women?
2. Do you think men and women have equal career opportunities?
3. Do you think women are as successful as men in the business world? Why or why not?

VOCABULARY PREVIEW

◆ **Match each word with the correct definition.**

1	inequality •	• a.	to prevent or slow down
2	trait •	• b.	to cause (something) to stop happening for a time
3	inhibit •	• c.	in a way that is intended or planned; purposely
4	interrupt •	• d.	a quality that makes one person or thing different from another
5	diverse •	• e.	lack of equality; a situation in which some people have an unfair advantage over others
6	deliberately •	• f.	made up of people or things that are different from each other

THE GLASS CEILING

Track 48

What qualities do managers look for in leaders?

Many professional women fear that they can never make it to the top. Even though they work hard, few reach the most powerful positions in business. We call this the "glass ceiling." Although women are told they are equal to men, there seems to be an unseen **barrier**[1] preventing them from rising higher. Among the Fortune Global 500—the world's 500 biggest companies ranked by *Fortune* magazine—only forty-one had women as CEOs in 2020. But why? There are different theories.

Some feminists put most of the blame on sex discrimination. Attitudes toward women almost certainly **inhibit** women's progress in some ways. For example, women are generally thought of as more caring and less **aggressive**[2] than men. But high-level managers tend to think aggressiveness and competitiveness are positive **traits**

[1] **barrier** *n.* something that prevents or blocks movement
[2] **aggressive** *adj.* forceful; ready and willing to fight, argue, etc.

for leaders. A study in 2018 found that women who **deliberately** showed these "masculine" traits at **appropriate**[3] times were more successful. Other research has found that most people link leadership with qualities that are **typically**[4] associated with men, such as being decisive. Qualities that are usually considered more feminine, such as cooperativeness, are viewed as less important. Although these attitudes can be considered sexist stereotypes, the researchers found they are held by both men and women.

But sexist attitudes may not be the whole explanation. Some people point to the choices women make as reasons why they are less likely to hold the most high-powered, high-paying jobs. Most women become mothers in their twenties and early thirties, an event that may **interrupt** their careers. Whether it is fair or not, having children is usually a greater **burden**[5] on a mother than a father in terms of time and effort—and that means less time at the office. Research shows that women tend to work fewer hours than men in the same industry and are more likely to choose part-time over full-time jobs. The trend toward companies giving more paid time off to both new mothers and new fathers might help correct this **inequality**. However, women are much more likely than men to seek work in areas such as **human resources**[6], which rarely lead them to the highest levels in business. Some argue that most women simply prefer jobs that allow them more time with their families. But critics say that sexism in the **corporate**[7] world discourages women from trying to compete in it.

Despite the debate about why there are few women heading corporations, most people agree that equal opportunity and more **diverse** business leadership are good goals. And women are making progress in breaking through the glass ceiling. Although forty-one female CEOs in the Fortune Global 500 is a low number, it is also the highest ever reached. As more women take top positions in the corporate world, they **pave the way**[8] for others to do the same.

Reading Time: ______ minutes ______ seconds 468 words

What trend might help working mothers?

3	**appropriate**	*adj.*	right or suitable
4	**typically**	*adv.*	in most cases; usually
5	**burden**	*n.*	something that is difficult or that causes worry; a load
6	**human resources**	*n.*	the department within an organization that deals with the people who work there
7	**corporate**	*adj.*	involving or associated with corporations
8	**pave the way**	*idiom*	to make it easier for something to happen

READING COMPREHENSION

A **Mark each statement as true (T) or false (F) according to the reading.**

1. ______ The "glass ceiling" refers to the difficulty women have in reaching the top in business.
2. ______ Forty-one percent of Fortune Global 500 CEOs in 2020 were women.
3. ______ Research shows that typically feminine traits are valued in leaders.
4. ______ There is disagreement about the reasons for the glass ceiling.
5. ______ More women than men decide to work in human resources.

B **Choose the best answer according to the reading.**

1 What is the main topic of the reading? TOPIC

a. The challenges faced by women in the workplace
b. Why women choose different types of work than men
c. The reason masculine traits are beneficial in business
d. How company policies are creating more equal offices

2 In paragraph 3, the word *industry* means ______. VOCABULARY

a. steady effort
b. making products in factories
c. a type of work or business
d. a field of study

3 Which is NOT true of working women? DETAIL

a. They are more likely than men to choose part-time work.
b. They work as many hours as men in similar jobs.
c. They do more of the work of taking care of children than men.
d. They often choose jobs that are unlikely to lead to promotion.

4 Which statement is the writer most likely to agree with? INFERENCE

a. Sex discrimination is not a major problem in business.
b. Women should not take time off when they have kids.
c. Most men do not want to remove the glass ceiling.
d. There will be more female CEOs in the future.

C **Look for the answers in the reading and write them on the lines.**

1 What is the Fortune Global 500?

____

2 What are two goals that most people agree on?

____

SUMMARY

Fill in the blanks with the phrases in the box.

good for leaders	more female CEOs	500 biggest
part-time jobs	mothers' time	were most successful

The "glass ceiling": a barrier preventing women from reaching the top (e.g., only forty-one female CEOs in the 1 ______________ companies)

Sex Discrimination

- "Feminine" traits like caring not considered 2 ______________
- Study: women who showed both male and female traits at different times 3 ______________

Other Factors

- Children take more of 4 ______________
- Women work fewer hours, have more 5 ______________
- Women's choices or sexism?

- 6 ______________ now than ever; they are paving the way for others

VOCABULARY PRACTICE

Fill in the blanks with the words in the box. Change the form if necessary.

diverse	trait	inequality	inhibit	interrupt	deliberately

1. Some governments try to reduce economic ______________ by taxing the rich and giving money to the poor.
2. Good habits like washing your hands often help to ______________ the spread of disease.
3. I ______________ arrived thirty minutes early for the presentation so I could get a good seat.
4. We must protect the ______________ plant and animal life of the Amazon, which may contain about half of the world's species.
5. Marjorie had to ______________ the meeting in order to take an important phone call.
6. Eye color is a physical ______________ that people get from their parents.

SPEAKING

8B Job Ad

A Vocabulary

Look up the pronunciations and meanings of the words below.

certificate

retirement

interact

technical

paperwork

promotion

overtime

outstanding

B Authentic Text

1. **Read the job advertisement and fill in the blanks with the correct words from activity A. Then listen and check your answers.** Track 49

Full-time Medical Assistant – Hope Valley Hospital

At Hope Valley Hospital, we pride ourselves in providing ❶ ______________ medical care to our community. We are seeking a responsible, flexible, and quick learner to join our staff. The position starts on November 10th. You will be working in eight-hour shifts, five days a week. Candidates must have a Medical Assistant ❷ ______________. Strong ❸ ______________ and communication skills are required, as medical assistants frequently ❹ ______________ with patients. Regular duties include greeting and checking out patients, handling ❺ ______________, and helping doctors and nurses with medical procedures. Every so often, we will also ask you to answer the phone and schedule appointments.

We are offering a competitive salary, opportunities to work ❻ ______________ for bonus pay, chances for ❼ ______________, a generous ❽ ______________ plan, and other benefits. To apply, send a resume and cover letter to humanresources@hopevalley.org.

Brief note

Duties (singular: *duty*) are things that you must do as part of your job.

2. Match the words with the correct definitions.

1. position •	• a. something extra that is given to employees in addition to their usual pay
2. flexible •	• b. a medical treatment or operation
3. procedure •	• c. a job
4. benefit •	• d. extra money that is given to an employee, especially for hard work
5. shift •	• e. able to change or be changed easily according to the situation
6. bonus •	• f. the scheduled period of time during which a person works

C In Your World

What's important in a job?

Which of the following are the most important to you in a job? Rank them from 1 (most) to 5 (least). Then discuss your ranking with a partner.

_____ high salary _____ good benefits _____ flexible hours

_____ chances for promotion _____ interacting with people

D Grammar

Present tenses; adverbs of frequency

simple present vs. present continuous			
simple present		**present continuous**	
routine actions or habits	**Do** medical assistants **help** doctors?	actions now	She can't talk now; she**'s working**.
facts	"Outstanding" **means** "excellent."	temporary facts	We **are seeking** new staff members right now.
scheduled future events	The position **starts** on November 10th.	future plans	**Are** you **going** back to college next year?
action verbs vs. stative verbs			
Action verbs describe actions and can be used in the continuous form.		*eat, play, watch, achieve, interact, improve, explain, monitor, experience, drive, work, plan, shop, laugh, seek, communicate*	
Stative verbs describe states and are NOT usually used in the continuous form.		*be, appreciate, feel, believe, include, have, seem, remember, mean, understand, know, own, like, love, hate, forget, wish*	

1. If the sentence is correct, write OK. If it is incorrect, underline the error and write the correction on the line.

1. Tom isn't coming to the meeting because he does paperwork. ____________
2. I work in a different department this week. ____________
3. Your flight arrives at 3:35 p.m. tomorrow. ____________
4. Are you believing that you are right for this position? ____________

adverbs of frequency						
Adverbs of frequency state how often something happens and are often used with simple tenses.						
never	hardly ever	seldom/rarely	sometimes	often	usually	always
0%			**50%**			**100**
once in a while / every so often / occasionally			regularly / frequently			all the time
One-word adverbs of frequency (and *hardly ever*) most often come before the verb, but after the verb *be*.						
*Salespeople **frequently** interact with customers.*		*We **hardly ever** see her.*		*She's **sometimes** busy.*		
Multiple-word adverbs of frequency usually come at the beginning or end of the sentence. *Sometimes*, *occasionally*, *frequently*, *often*, and *usually* may also come at the beginning or the end of the sentence:						
***Once in a while**, he misses work.*		*I'll ask for help **every so often**.*		*She's busy **sometimes**.*		

2. Circle the correct word(s).

1. Doctors interact with patients (usually / all the time).
2. My work hours were (usually / every so often) flexible.
3. (Sometimes / Seldom) she works overtime at the office.
4. His work is (always / every so often) outstanding.
5. I have technical questions (frequently / hardly ever).
6. (Never / Occasionally), they work the late shift.

E Use the Language

Writing a Job Ad

Think of a job that you would like to have in the future. On a separate sheet of paper, write a short advertisement for that job. Include the following information:

- Duties
- Necessary education and other qualifications
- Salary and benefits
- Usual working hours

Share your advertisement with the class.

WRITING

1. Where can you find job ads?

2. What is the best way to find a job? What qualifications do you need to find a job you want?

SUPPLEMENTAL READING

Women in World Politics

Track 50

Margaret Thatcher was one of the most famous female politicians of the 20th century. She knew that the world was watching her and judging all women as leaders. When she became the United Kingdom's first female prime minister in 1979, she said, "A great deal, I think, of the future of women at the top will depend on how I do." Even those who disagree with her admit that she was an effective political leader. Thatcher was re-elected twice. Her strength and determination earned her the nickname "Iron Lady." Since Thatcher, many other women have become leaders of countries. But as with female CEOs, they remain a small minority.

Some have argued that women make especially good leaders. Chandrika Kumaratunga became president of Sri Lanka in 1994. She felt women brought certain advantages to politics. "Where there is a dedicated, honest, and sincere woman somewhere at the top, she can bring in a much more human touch and a much more practical approach to problems, and that's very important in politics," Kumaratunga said.

Like Thatcher, however, successful female politicians are not always seen as having a different, "feminine" leadership style. Angela Merkel led Germany from 2005 to 2021 as its first female head of state. She was one of the longest-serving and most powerful leaders in her country's history. Merkel and her supporters never focused on her sex but rather on her intelligence and talents. As one journalist put it, she "perhaps made the idea of a woman leading her country feel normal."

Fill in the blanks with information from the reading.

1. Margaret Thatcher was the first female ______________________ of the UK.
2. According to ______________________, women's traits are especially valuable in politics.
3. Angela Merkel's supporters talk about her ______________________, not her gender.

EXTENSION Talk or Write About It

Why do you think there are more powerful men than women in business and government? Do you think there will ever be as many women as men in the top positions? Why or why not?

UNIT 9-1 Media

Scan for Audio

Pre-Reading Questions

◆ **Think about the following questions.**

1. When and how do you listen to music?
2. When and how did people listen to music in the past?
3. How do you think people will listen to music twenty years from now?

VOCABULARY PREVIEW

◆ **Match each word with the correct definition.**

1. dominant	a. causing or relating to a great or complete change
2. swap	b. higher in quality
3. compact	c. smaller than other things of the same kind
4. revolutionary	d. a form or system of communication or entertainment
5. superior	e. to exchange for something else
6. medium (pl. media)	f. the most common; the most important

The Evolution of Music Media

Track 51

Chances are you sometimes listen to music on the radio. Maybe you've downloaded your favorite songs to your phone, but you also stream the latest music online. And your parents and grandparents probably have some old CDs and **vinyl**[1] records. These days, we have so many music **formats**[2] to choose from. How did we get so many choices? Well, ever since the music industry was born, companies have been trying to make it more **convenient**[3] for people to play their favorite music when and where they choose.

Vinyl records were the first **medium** for commercial music **reproduction**[4]. This was the most popular music format from the 1950s until the 1990s. The standard kind of vinyl record was the LP. "LP" **stands for**[5] "long play," as these were the first records that could continuously play twenty minutes or more of music. Of course, no one could carry LPs around and listen to them on the bus or subway. Record players, or turntables, were too big. So teenagers usually gathered at a friend's house, where they listened to records together. In that way, music was a social activity.

Why were the most common type of vinyl records called "LPs"?

1	**vinyl**	*n.*	flexible plastic material
2	**format**	*n.*	a form; a layout
3	**convenient**	*adj.*	easy to use
4	**reproduction**	*n.*	the act of copying something
5	**stand for**	*v.*	to mean; to signify

In the 1970s, Sony began selling a **revolutionary** device: the Walkman. This **portable**[6] device allowed music lovers to take their music anywhere and listen to it privately—even in public places. The Walkman played **compact** audiocassette tapes, which were a new kind of music format.

Underline one reason why CDs did not immediately replace other music media.

Cassettes lost popularity with the introduction of the compact disc, or CD. CD technology was released in the United States in 1983, but it took until the mid-1990s for this format to dominate the music market. One reason is that CDs and CD players were fairly expensive at first. Also, many people thought vinyl records had a **superior** sound. In fact, there are still some LP enthusiasts who prefer listening to records.

At the start of the 21st century, CDs held the largest **portion**[7] of the market. But by 2007, sales of CDs had fallen sharply as people **swapped** them for the new digital format, MP3. By **converting**[8] music to MP3 files, users could store several times more music on a CD. But more important was the 1997 invention of the MP3 player, and, a few years after that, the smartphone—**devices**[9] that could hold thousands of songs. They allowed users to buy music online, download it, and listen to it immediately. Change didn't stop there, of course. In recent years, online streaming on platforms such as YouTube and Spotify has been replacing downloadable MP3s as the **dominant** medium in places with reliable Internet access. In 2018, YouTube reported that more than a billion people streamed music on their app each month. Both YouTube and Spotify now allow users to access ad-free music streaming for a monthly **fee**[10], and the popularity of these services is growing fast.

No one knows what the future holds for music media. But think about how many new formats have been invented in the past century. We can probably expect another revolutionary new way to listen to music before very long.

Reading Time: _______ minutes _______ seconds 508 words

6	**portable**	*adj.*	easy to carry or move around
7	**portion**	*n.*	a part of a larger amount
8	**convert**	*v.*	to change (something) into a different form
9	**device**	*n.*	an object or machine made for some special purpose
10	**fee**	*n.*	an amount of money that must be paid

READING COMPREHENSION

A Mark each statement as true (T) or false (F) according to the reading.

1. _____ At the start of the 21st century, LPs were the dominant music medium.
2. _____ The Walkman played a new type of music medium.
3. _____ CDs became the standard music medium in the 1990s.
4. _____ Some people think LPs have a better sound than CDs.
5. _____ Streaming has replaced other media worldwide.

B Choose the best answer according to the reading.

1. Which is true about vinyl records? **DETAIL**
   a. They replaced an earlier commercial format.
   b. They helped make music portable.
   c. They were played on turntables.
   d. They replaced the audiocassette tape.

2. What can be inferred about audiocassettes? **INFERENCE**
   a. They made music less of a social activity.
   b. They were only produced by Sony.
   c. Many people still prefer them to MP3s.
   d. All of the above

3. In paragraph 4, the word *enthusiasts* means ______. **VOCABULARY**
   a. fans
   b. brands
   c. makers
   d. experts

4. When were compact discs first introduced in the US? **DETAIL**
   a. In the 1950s
   b. In the 1970s
   c. In the 1980s
   d. In the 1990s

C Fill in the blanks with information from the reading.

1. LPs were not a portable music medium because __________________________ were too big.
2. The invention of __________________________ made audiocassettes less popular.
3. One reason that CDs were slow to dominate the market was that they were initially pretty __________________________.

SUMMARY

Fill in the blanks with the phrases in the box.

made music portable	buy music online	for decades
by 2007	streaming services	more convenient

As music media evolve, listening to music becomes 1 ____________.

Past

LPs

- First commercial medium
- Dominated 2 ____________ ____________
- Made music social

Audiocassettes

- Sony introduced the Walkman in the 1970s
- 3 ____________ ____________

Present

CDs

- Became popular in mid-90s
- Sales fell sharply 4 ____________

MP3s

- Made storage easy
- Allows users to 5 ____________ and enjoy it immediately

Future

- 6 ____________ are starting to replace MP3 downloads
- Other revolutionary ideas?

VOCABULARY PRACTICE

Fill in the blanks with the words in the box. Change the form if necessary.

superior	medium	compact	swap	dominant	revolutionary

1. Only ____________ cars can fit into this parking space.
2. Tourism is the ____________ industry in several Caribbean countries.
3. The invention of rock and roll marked a ____________ change in popular music.
4. It is worthwhile to pay more for quality shoes because their ____________ materials will last longer.
5. Since you don't like sitting by the window and I do, we should ____________ seats.
6. In the 1940s, radio was still the most important ____________ of mass communication.

SPEAKING

9A What Are You Watching?

A Warm-up

Talk about the questions as a class.

1. What was the last movie you watched on TV or on the phone?
2. Where and how did you watch it?

B Multi-Text

1. **Read the texts. Then answer the questions.** Track 52

Text 1

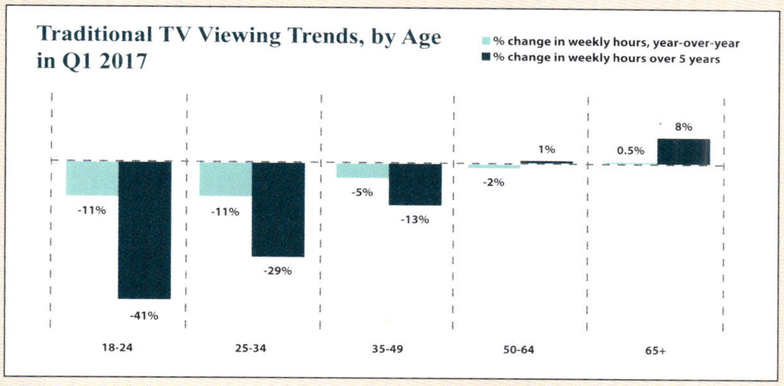

Talk about

1. Which age group's TV viewing has changed the most over five years? Is this group watching more traditional TV or less?
2. What two streaming services are mentioned in Text 2?
3. What does the writer of Text 3 think about recent superhero movies.

Brief note

Broadcast networks are TV companies that show programs over a large area.

Text 2

Companies such as Netflix have changed the entertainment industry. Broadcast networks have more competition now than ever before. Convenient streaming services allow users to enjoy their favorite programs on several devices. In the past, streaming services worked with major networks and studios. These services showed content that people had already seen on TV or at the movie theater. But many companies are starting to change this. Netflix and Amazon are two streaming services that are developing their own programs and films. They are able to draw talented and well-known celebrities. For example, the award-winning actor John Arthur Lithgow plays a supporting role in the Netflix series *The Crown*.

Brief note

Streaming services are companies like Netflix that allow customers to view movies and TV series on the Internet.

Text 3

There's a huge problem in Hollywood right now: a lack of creativity. Every year, there are more and more sequels. Original films seem to be dying out. Take superhero movies, for example. They've dominated the movie industry since *Iron Man* in 2008. But the quality of these films started to decline after the surprise summer hit *The Avengers* in 2012. Since then, the same stories are being told over and over, and it's getting boring. The same criticism applies to other movie series, such as *the Fast and the Furious*, *Transformers*, and *Star Wars*. Hollywood keeps re-making past movies and TV shows. Many characters and plots that we see at the theater are already familiar. Why can't movie studios come up with fresh stories?

2. **Decide which text each question refers to. Choose 1, 2, or 3 and write it on the line.**

Which text…

discusses a problem with today's movie industry?	______
tells you how the TV habits of young people have changed recently?	______
complains about a lack of new ideas?	______
states that Internet companies are making their own shows and movies?	______
mentions that famous people are working with new companies?	______

3. **Cross out the two false statements. Write the number of the correct text (1, 2, or 3) next to the true statements.**

1. ______ Streaming services used to show things that people had already seen.
2. ______ Hollywood has been showing a lot of creativity in recent years.
3. ______ Most age groups have been watching less traditional TV.
4. ______ Superhero movies have been popular since 2008.
5. ______ Netflix has made a series with a well-known star.
6. ______ Superhero movies have been getting worse since 2012.
7. ______ People under the age of 50 have been watching more TV lately.

C Vocabulary

1. **Circle the word that is closest in meaning to the word in bold.**

1. **major**	rich	old	important	creative
2. **decline**	decrease	depart	design	delay
3. **familiar**	fun	known	liked	right
4. **fresh**	popular	weird	clean	new
5. **creativity**	imagination	ambition	presentation	education

2. Match the words and phrases with the correct definitions.

1. studio	•	•	a. statements about the quality of someone or something, often bad
2. star	•	•	b. many times; repeatedly
3. over and over	•	•	c. a movie, book, etc. that continues the story from an earlier one
4. criticism	•	•	d. a movie or TV company or a place where movies or TV shows are made
5. apply	•	•	e. to be one of the main characters in a movie, play, TV show, etc.
6. sequel	•	•	f. special and interesting because of being different from others
7. original	•	•	g. to affect or relate to a certain person or situation

D In Your World

Talk About Film and TV

Discuss the following questions with a partner.

1. What movie have you watched over and over again? Why? Who stars in it? What is it about?

2. How much time do you spend watching movies or TV in a typical week? Which do you watch more, traditional TV or streaming services?

3. Have you seen any of the shows or movies mentioned in activity B? What do you think about them?

4. Do you agree with the writer in activity B who says that most Hollywood movies today aren't original? Why or why not?

MEMO

WRITING

1. What kinds of OTT (Over the Top) services are you subscribing to?

2. Do you prefer watching movies at home or seeing them at the cinema? Why?

Can Musicians Still Make Money?

Track 53

The technology we use to access and listen to music is constantly evolving. And while such changes usually benefit music fans, they don't always help musicians. When the MP3 format became popular, people quickly discovered how to download music without paying for it. Piracy—getting and sharing music illegally—reduces the income that musicians make from their work. Now streaming services are reducing musical artists' profits even further.

Consumers can pay a monthly fee for streaming services that allow them to listen to an unlimited amount of music online. As a result, fewer MP3 files are being purchased and downloaded. Internet music services must pay royalties (fees) to record companies in order to play the songs that these companies own. But most of that money is kept by the record companies, and little is left over for the musicians.

One songwriter and keyboardist kept track of his royalties from streaming over three months. His songs were played more than 14,000 times—but he made only $35.09. Even major stars have similar experiences. Members of the British bands Led Zeppelin and Radiohead have participated in a government investigation of streaming services and their profits.

Of course, famous musicians can make a lot of money in other ways: by giving huge concerts, selling their songs for ads, and so on. But new and lesser-known musicians do not have these options. It is easier than ever for young musicians to share their work with the world. But with piracy and streaming, it is getting harder for them to make a living from it.

Fill in the blanks with information from the reading.

1 Getting and sharing music illegally is called ________________.

2 The fees paid for playing songs owned by ________________ are called royalties.

3 It is becoming ________________ for new musicians to make money from their music.

EXTENSION Talk or Write About It

What is your preferred way to get and listen to music? Why?

UNIT 9-2 Media

Pre-Reading Questions

◆ **Think about the following questions.**

1. Which video-streaming services do you use? What do you watch?
2. Do you watch regular television with your family? Why or why not?
3. What do you think are the positive and negative aspects of streaming services?

Scan for Audio

VOCABULARY PREVIEW

◆ **Match each word with the correct definition.**

1 fringe •	• a. against or opposed to
2 meaningful •	• b. not belonging to the main part of a group, activity, or subject
3 reinforce •	• c. useful, serious, or important
4 facilitate •	• d. to help happen or make possible
5 availability •	• e. the measure of how possible it is to get or use something
6 anti- •	• f. to make an object or idea stronger; to support it

Home
Watch
Search

Streaming Services: Helpful or Harmful?

Track 54

Video-streaming services such as Netflix, Amazon Prime Video, and YouTube have made finding things to watch easier than ever before. Most people praise these services for their convenience. However, there are consequences to streaming services that need to be taken into account. For instance, the reliability of the information on shows is starting to decrease as different companies apply different standards to their content. Streaming services are also problematic because their **curation**[1] systems often keep people from experiencing new genres and ideas. And worst of all, streaming services can even **facilitate** the decline of social relationships.

There are plenty of great shows on streaming platforms. Unfortunately, though, there are also a lot of bad ones. And by bad, I mean harmful. These shows can incite violence, promote bad science, or spread **biased**[2] journalism. To illustrate, a show that affirms **pseudoscientific**[3] practices like energy healing and the use of medical mediums (people who claim they speak with spirits for medical advice) as alternatives to science-based medicine can cause lots of unintentional harm. Granted, these shows aren't a recent phenomenon. They existed on traditional **broadcast**[4] television as well. But the growth in the frequency and **availability** of this type of content is rising because of streaming services.

Why do most people like using streaming services?

Streaming services don't just host shows. They also offer recommendations based on your viewing history. This can be very convenient but also very limiting. Platforms that utilize targeted advertising and curation tend to direct users toward content focused on a very narrow set of topics

1	**curation**	*n.*	the selection of content to be included as part of a list or collection
2	**biased**	*adj.*	showing unfair ideas about something based only on opinion
3	**pseudoscientific**	*adj.*	against proven facts and science, but claiming to be true
4	**broadcast**	*n.*	the act of sending out radio or television signals

and viewpoints. For some, this goes unnoticed or is seen as a minor inconvenience. But this type of targeting can become harmful when it leads a person down a path towards **fringe** groups such as **anti**-vaxxers (people opposed to **vaccinations**[5]) and then continues to provide content that **reinforces** these **radical**[6] ideas.

Although some criticize traditional broadcast television for its inconvenience, it does provide people with common ground. People **bond**[7] by watching television together and talking about their favorite shows. Broadcast television gives families a reason to gather together and allows friends and coworkers to connect over shared interests. Sadly, though, streaming services have contributed to the decline in these kinds of **meaningful** **interactions**[8]. Since streamed shows are available **on demand**[9], there's no reason to wait to watch them with friends or family. There's also no reason to go out of your way to see the first airing or to catch a **rerun**[10]. Smart devices allow every family member to watch whatever they want, whenever they want. While convenient in some cases, this works to divide a family's tastes and interests further.

At a glance, video-streaming services are incredible. They're so convenient. They **revitalize**[11] canceled shows and keep us from having to wait for reruns. But every rose has its thorn. The time has come to think and act responsibly about what we view and how we view it.

Q **Underline two examples of pseudoscience.**

Q **Underline two examples of tools used by platforms to direct viewers to certain content.**

Reading Time: _______ minutes _______ seconds 478 words

[5] **vaccination** *n.* a treatment to produce immunity against a disease
[6] **radical** *adj.* extreme in words, beliefs, or actions
[7] **bond** *v.* to form a close relationship with someone
[8] **interaction** *n.* a moment when two or more people communicate or relate to each other
[9] **on demand** *adv.* being available whenever a viewer wants
[10] **rerun** *n.* a TV show or film that is repeated or shown again
[11] **revitalize** *v.* to bring back to life or help recover

READING COMPREHENSION

A Mark each statement as true (T) or false (F) according to the reading.

1. ______ The information in online shows is becoming more accurate.
2. ______ The number of pseudoscientific programs is increasing due to streaming services.
3. ______ Streaming services discourage viewers from watching fringe content.
4. ______ On-demand media provides people with common ground and shared experiences.
5. ______ Video-streaming services can bring old shows back to life.

B Choose the best answer according to the reading.

1. What is the main purpose of the reading? **PURPOSE**
   a. To recommend several of the best video-streaming services
   b. To provide advice on using video-streaming services wisely
   c. To discuss the disadvantages of video-streaming services
   d. To compare traditional broadcast media to streaming services

2. In paragraph 2, the word *They* refers to ______. **REFERENCE**
   a. streaming services
   b. science-based shows
   c. biased journalists
   d. pseudoscientific programs

3. What is a problem with curation? **DETAIL**
   a. It encourages people to view a wide range of shows.
   b. It encourages people to watch too much similar content.
   c. It encourages people to ask questions about society.
   d. It encourages people to learn about scientific theories.

4. Which statement would the writer most likely agree with? **INFERENCE**
   a. Content by fringe groups should be removed from streaming services.
   b. Viewers should avoid content recommended to them by streaming services.
   c. Families should make time to watch streaming or broadcast media together.
   d. Parents should not allow their children to use video-streaming services.

C Fill in the blanks with information from the reading.

1. Curation and ______________________ are used by streaming services to encourage viewers to watch certain content.
2. Some streamed shows suggest that pseudosciences like energy healing are a genuine ______________________ to science-based medicine.
3. Broadcast media provides people with ______________________. This means they have shared interests to talk about.

SUMMARY

An introductory sentence for a brief summary of the passage is given below. Choose three more sentences to complete the summary.

First Sentence: Although streaming services are incredibly convenient, they also have some negative effects.

1. They can make families lead very separate lives and cause people to become distant from one another.
2. In fact, in 2020, the largest streaming service, Netflix, announced it had 204 million users.
3. These include increasing the availability of content that contains biased news, false information, and pseudoscience.
4. Curation and targeted advertising often mean that viewers are exposed to a limited range of content.
5. Traditional broadcasters guess what we want to see, whereas streaming services allow us to watch what we are genuinely interested in.

VOCABULARY PRACTICE

Fill in the blanks with the words in the box. Change the form if necessary.

fringe	facilitate	availability	anti-	meaningful	reinforce

1. To ________________ the group discussion, I'll write some questions on the whiteboard.
2. Which people have had the most ________________ effect on your life?
3. One benefit of streaming services is the ________________ of whole box sets on demand.
4. Doing homework helps to ________________ what you learned in class.
5. The theory that the Earth is flat is a(n) ________________ idea.
6. Because viewers often watch alone, streaming services can be ________________social.

SPEAKING

9B Crime Report

A Vocabulary

Look up the pronunciation and meaning of the words below. Then listen. Track 55

escape

break into

trial

attack

police officer

prison

punish

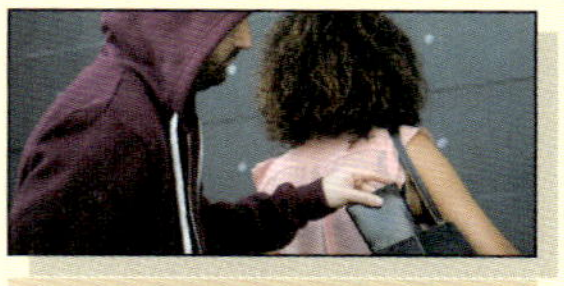
steal

Brief note

If someone is *suspected* of a crime, it means that people think he or she might have done it. A person who is suspected of a crime is called a *suspect*.

B Authentic Text

1. Read the news report and fill in the blanks with the correct words from activity A. Change the form if necessary. Then listen and check your answers. Track 56

On Saturday night, two men were arrested after a traffic stop. ❶ ________________ stopped a vehicle on Keystone Boulevard for going much faster than the speed limit. The driver began to answer the officers' questions. But he then ❷ ________________ one of the officers. Both men tried to ❸ ________________ by running away on foot. But the officers were quicker and caught the suspects after a fifteen-minute chase. Police later found $50,000 in cash inside the vehicle.

The two suspects were arrested, and police worked to find out how they had gotten the money. Video was found from a security camera at a nearby bank. It seems to show the men breaking into an ATM to ❹ ________________ the cash. That is by far the biggest theft from an ATM in local history.

Both suspects are being kept in the city jail while they wait for their ❺ ________________. This crime can be ❻ ________________ by a maximum of ten years in ❼ ________________, although the punishment may be less serious if it is the criminal's first crime. We will continue to report on this story as it develops.

Brief note

Chase is both a verb and a noun. It means to run after someone to try to catch him or her, or the act of doing this.

2. Match the words and phrases with the correct definitions.

1. break into	•	•	a. the largest (amount) that is allowed or possible
2. arrest	•	•	b. an illegal act
3. theft	•	•	c. the action or crime of stealing something
4. crime	•	•	d. a place where criminals or suspected criminals are kept
5. criminal	•	•	e. a person who has committed an illegal action
6. maximum	•	•	f. to get into (a locked building, car, etc.), usually to steal something
7. jail	•	•	g. to take (someone) away because he or she is suspected of a crime

Brief note

Jail and *prison* have similar meanings. The word *jail* usually refers to a place where suspects stay for a short time after they are arrested. A *prison* is a place where criminals are kept for a long time as punishment.

C In Your World

Talk About the News

Discuss the following questions with a partner.

1. Do you pay much attention to the news? How (by reading online news, watching TV, etc.)?

2. Are you interested in news stories about crime? Why or why not?

3. Talk about a crime that was recently reported in the local news. What happened? What have the police done about it?

D Grammar

Comparisons

comparative adjectives and adverbs		
one-syllable adj./adv.	**short adj./adv. ending in -y**	**other adj. / adv.**
+ *-er* (*than ~*)	*y* + *ier* (*than ~*)	*more* + adj./adv. (*than ~*)
The officers were **quicker**. She's going **faster than** the speed limit.	She seems **friendlier than** her brother. They opened the bank **earlier** today.	The punishment should be **more serious**. We must take theft **more seriously**.
superlative adjectives and adverbs		
one-syllable adj./adv.	**short adj./adv. ending in -y**	**other adj. / adv.**
+ *-est*	*y* + *iest*	*most* + adj./adv.
It was **the biggest** theft in history. He drives **the fastest**.	That's **the ugliest** building in town. What stores open **the earliest**?	What's **the most serious** crime of all? What crime happens **the most often**?
Irregular: *good/well – better – best*	*bad/badly – worse – worst*	*far – further/farther – furthest/farthest*

1. Complete the sentences. Use the given words and any other words that are needed.

1. That's ______________________ idea I've ever heard! (*silly*)
2. What's the ______________________ type of crime in this city? (*common*)
3. I think that he should stay in prison ______________________ five years. (*long*)

comparison to a lesser degree	
comparative	**superlative**
less + adj./adv. (*than* ~) = *not as* adj./adv. (*as* ~)	*the least* + adj./adv.
Our neighborhood is **less dangerous than** that one. = Our neighborhood is**n't as dangerous as** that one.	What's **the least dangerous** neighborhood in town? I think social media reports the news **the least accurately**.
intensifiers	
before comparatives: *even, (so) much, a lot, far*	**before superlatives:** *by far*
Our neighborhood is **a lot less dangerous** than that one. Newspapers report the news **far better** than TV.	This was **by far the biggest** theft in local history. The Internet reports the news **by far the least accurately**.

2. Underline the mistake and write the correction on the line. (There may be more than one possible correction.)

1. What is least safe way to travel? ______________________
2. Being an office worker is not exciting as being a police officer. ______________________
3. Crime is very more common in the city than in the country. ______________________

E Use the Language

Interview with a Police Officer

1. Work with a partner. Imagine that you are a journalist reporting on the story in activity B. What would you ask the police officers who arrested the two men? Write at least three questions.

____

____

____

____

2. Role-play an interview. One partner is a journalist, and the other is one of the police officers from activity B. Practice the interview, and then perform it for the class.

WRITING

1. What current news stories are you most interested in? Why are they interesting to you?

2. Where do you get your news from? TV, newspapers, or the Internet? Why do you prefer that method?

SUPPLEMENTAL READING

From Courtroom to Living Room

Track 57

True-crime documentaries can be a fascinating look into a country's justice system. They can also be a useful tool to bring the public's attention to injustices. New evidence revealed in several documentaries has even led to innocent people being released from prison. *The Thin Blue Line*, released in 1988, focused on one such case. It told the story of Randall Dale Adams, a man imprisoned for the murder of a police officer in Texas. The documentary called the handling of Adams's case into question. A year after the documentary's release, Adams was granted a new trial, and his charges were dropped.

Thanks to the growth of video-streaming services, more true-crime documentaries are being produced than ever before. Netflix has created several popular true-crime shows, including *Making a Murderer*, which details the trial and conviction of Steven Avery. After watching the first season of the show, which questioned the evidence against Avery, a viewer named Kathleen Zellner decided to help Avery change the court's decision. Zellner is a lawyer, and her efforts to get Avery released became the focus of the documentary's second season.

Helping to build public awareness of injustices is definitely a benefit of having more true-crime shows. But are there any disadvantages? Perhaps there are. As streaming platforms compete to produce fresh content and gain more viewers, the quality of research into such criminal cases will likely begin to fall. As a result, courts might find themselves flooded with attempts to free people who are, in fact, guilty.

Fill in the blanks with information from the reading.

1. *The Thin Blue Line* and *Making a Murderer* are true-crime ______________ that have helped draw attention to possible injustice.
2. Kathleen Zellner was originally a(n) ______________ of *Making a Murderer*, but went on to appear in the second season.
3. Shows like these help to increase ______________, but they could also make the legal system less reliable.

EXTENSION Talk or Write About It

What do you like about streaming services? What kinds of problems might they cause?

UNIT 10-1 Culture

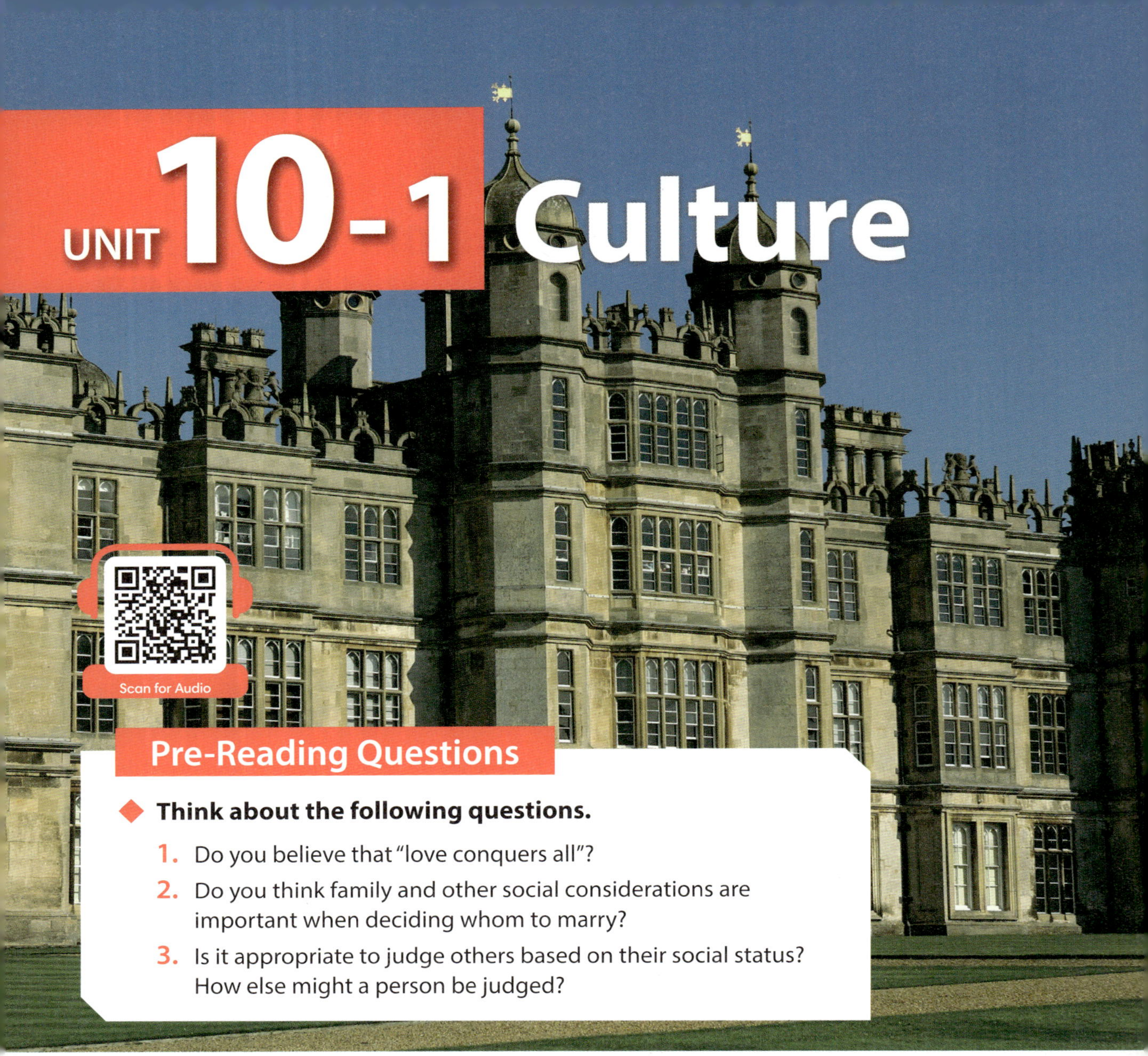

Scan for Audio

Pre-Reading Questions

◆ **Think about the following questions.**

1. Do you believe that "love conquers all"?
2. Do you think family and other social considerations are important when deciding whom to marry?
3. Is it appropriate to judge others based on their social status? How else might a person be judged?

VOCABULARY PREVIEW

◆ **Match each word with the correct definition.**

1. admission	a. without being aware
2. inferiority	b. the period of time during which something lasts
3. evident	c. the act of confessing something
4. disturbance	d. the state of being lower in rank or quality
5. duration	e. obvious
6. unconsciously	f. the state of being disturbed; the act of disturbing

Pride and Prejudice

Track 58

by Jane Austen

[excerpted and adapted]

Elizabeth was suddenly **roused**[1] by the sound of the doorbell, and her spirits were a little fluttered by the idea of its being Colonel Fitzwilliam himself. He had once before called late in the evening and might now again have come to inquire particularly after her. But this idea was soon **banished**[2], and her spirits were very differently affected when, to her utter amazement, she saw Mr. Darcy walk into the room. In a hurried manner, he immediately began an inquiry after her health, imputing his visit to a wish of hearing if she felt better. She answered him with cold civility. He sat down for a few moments, then got up and walked around the room, which surprised Elizabeth, who said nothing.

Was Elizabeth pleased to see Darcy at the door? How do you know?

After a silence of several minutes, he came toward her in an agitated manner and said, "In vain I have struggled, and it will not do. My feelings will not be **repressed**[3], and you must allow me to tell you how **ardently**[4] I admire and love you."

Elizabeth's astonishment at his **admission** was so great that she stared, **colored**[5], doubted, and was silent. Darcy considered this sufficient encouragement; and so, he continued to tell her all he felt and had long felt for her. He spoke well, but there were feelings besides those of the heart that he detailed. And he was not more eloquent on the subject of tenderness than of pride. He dwelt on his sense of her **inferiority**, and also on the family obstacles which stood in their way, and told her that his better judgment had wrestled with his feelings.

In spite of her deeply rooted dislike for Darcy, Elizabeth could not be **insensible**[6] to the compliment of such a powerful man's affection, and though her intentions did not vary for an instant, she was sorry for the pain he was about to receive until, roused to resentment by his insensitive words, she

What emotions does Elizabeth experience as Darcy talks?

1	**rouse**	*v.*	to awaken or excite into action
2	**banish**	*v.*	to expel; to send or drive away
3	**repress**	*v.*	to hold in by self-control
4	**ardently**	*adv.*	with great warmth of feeling
5	**color**	*v.*	to blush
6	**insensible**	*adj.*	unaware of; unmindful

lost her compassion and became angry. She tried, however, to compose herself to answer him patiently, once he had finished talking.

He concluded by telling her of the strength of his love for her, which, in spite of all his **endeavors**[7], he had found impossible to conquer, and with his expression of hope that it would now be rewarded by her acceptance of his hand in marriage. As he said this, she could easily see that he had no doubt that she would answer affirmatively. He spoke of apprehension and anxiety, but his **countenance**[8] expressed real security that she would accept him.

This further exasperated her, and when he ceased talking, the color rose into her cheeks and she said, "In such cases as this, it is, I believe, the established mode to express a sense of obligation for the sentiments avowed, however unequally they may be returned. It is natural that obligation should be felt, and if I could feel gratitude I would now thank you. But I cannot—I have never desired your good opinion, and you have certainly **bestowed**[9] it most unwillingly. I am sorry to have caused you pain. It has been most **unconsciously** done and, I hope, will be of short **duration**. These feelings, which, you tell me, have long prevented the acknowledgment of your regard, will surely help you overcome your love for me, especially after what you have expressed as your true opinions of me and my family."

How did Elizabeth's response make Mr. Darcy feel? Underline the words.

Mr. Darcy, who was leaning against the **mantelpiece**[10] with his eyes fixed on her face, seemed to catch her words with both resentment and surprise. His complexion became pale with anger, and the **disturbance** of his mind was visible in every feature. He was struggling for the appearance of **composure**[11] and would not open his lips till he believed himself to have attained it.

The pause made Elizabeth feel dreadful, and at length, with a voice full of forced calmness, he said, "And this is all the reply which I am to have the honor of expecting! I might, perhaps, wish to be informed why, with so little endeavor at civility, I am thus rejected. But it is of small importance."

"I might as well inquire," replied she, "why with so **evident** a desire of offending and insulting me, you chose to tell me that you liked me against your will, against your reason, and even against your character."

Reading Time: _______ minutes _______ seconds 725 words

7	**endeavor**	*n.*	an effort; an attempt
8	**countenance**	*n.*	expression of the face
9	**bestow**	*v.*	to give something as a gift or an honor
10	**mantelpiece**	*n.*	the shelf above a fireplace
11	**composure**	*n.*	self-possession and control of emotions

READING COMPREHENSION

A **Mark each statement as true (T) or false (F) according to the reading.**

1. ______ Elizabeth was hoping that it was Mr. Darcy at the door.
2. ______ Based on her thoughts, it is clear that Elizabeth respects and admires Mr. Darcy.
3. ______ Mr. Darcy feels superior to Elizabeth and her family.
4. ______ Mr. Darcy was expecting Elizabeth to reject his proposal.
5. ______ Elizabeth refuses Mr. Darcy because she feels that he is too good for her.

B **Choose the best answer according to the reading.**

1. What is the excerpt mainly about? TOPIC
   a. Elizabeth's hatred of Mr. Darcy
   b. Mr. Darcy's arrogant assessment of Elizabeth
   c. Elizabeth's rejection of Mr. Darcy's marriage proposal
   d. How Elizabeth and Mr. Darcy try to disguise their feelings

2. Why did Elizabeth think that it would be Colonel Fitzwilliam at the door? DETAIL
   a. Because he had come to her house at the same time on a previous occasion
   b. Because he had called her to let her know that he would be stopping by
   c. Because he usually visited her at this time
   d. Because he was her husband, and she was expecting him to come home

3. The word *civility* in paragraph 1 is closest in meaning to ______. VOCABULARY
   a. politeness
   b. obligation
   c. respect
   d. surprise

4. It can be inferred from paragraphs 7 and 8 that Mr. Darcy ______. INFERENCE
   a. was not really surprised by her answer
   b. did not really care either way how she replied
   c. was not aware how rude and insensitive he was being
   d. was relieved because he had been forced by social pressure to ask

C **Fill in the blanks with information from the reading.**

1. After Mr. Darcy first entered and asked about Elizabeth's health, there was ______________________.
2. Elizabeth's main emotion at the moment when Mr. Darcy proposed marriage was ______________________.
3. Even though she disliked him, Elizabeth considered his proposal to be a ______________________ because he was so powerful.

SUMMARY

An introductory sentence for a brief summary of the passage is given below. Choose three more sentences to complete the summary.

First Sentence: Mr. Darcy arrived at Elizabeth's door and pretended he was there to ask about her health.

1. Elizabeth rejected his proposal, and Mr. Darcy stood silent at first, sincerely surprised and offended by her answer.
2. Elizabeth listened to Mr. Darcy's kind sentiments, and as she did so, she could imagine the wonderful life they would have together.
3. Darcy then professed his love for her, but Elizabeth grew upset because he spoke less of love than of pride and her inferiority to him.
4. As Mr. Darcy continued, his disrespect for her and her family made her angry, which turned to surprise when he asked her to marry him, confident that she would say yes.
5. After leaving her house, Mr. Darcy proceeded to his family home to discuss the night's events.
6. Mr. Darcy's remarks about her family made Elizabeth feel ashamed, and she apologized for their behavior.

VOCABULARY PRACTICE

Fill in the blanks with the words in the box. Change the form if necessary.

admission	disturbance	duration	inferiority	evident	unconsciously

1. Some very good restaurants are inexpensive, so don't assume that a low price is a sign of ____________________.
2. Painful experiences in childhood may lead to lasting emotional ____________________.
3. Everyone was shocked by Nicole's ____________________ that she had stolen the money.
4. My little brother cried for the entire ____________________ of the car ride to Grandma's house.
5. There are certain actions that people do ____________________ all the time, such as breathing, blinking, and swallowing.
6. Although the guests complimented their host enthusiastically, their true feelings about the food became ____________________ when they failed to finish it.

SPEAKING

10A Fashion

A Warm-up

Talk about the questions as a class.

What kinds of clothes are fashionable now? How have fashions changed in recent years?

B Authentic Text

1. Read and listen to the magazine article. Then answer the questions. Track 59

Brief note

A *subculture* is a group of people with similar beliefs, interests, etc., that are different from most other people's.

Paragraph 1

Fashion changes between seasons, between years, and between generations. Some generations can even be identified by their fashion. For example, most people have an idea of what the "hippie," "disco," and "grunge" generations wore. Fashion trends have many influences. Celebrities and subcultures have a huge effect on fashion trends. In addition, our individual attitudes and values can influence our fashion taste.

Paragraph 2

Celebrities are a major influence on fashion. For example, the model and actress Audrey Hepburn became a fashion icon in the 1960s. She helped popularize the "little black dress" in her film *Breakfast at Tiffany's*. Although the dress itself was created in the 1920s by designer Coco Chanel, Hepburn's film convinced many women to add it to their wardrobes. Besides actors, other celebrities have entered the fashion industry and achieved success. Musicians, such as Kanye West and Beyoncé Knowles, and athletes, such as David Beckham and Cristiano Ronaldo, have all created their own successful fashion brands.

Paragraph 3

Subcultures can also create fashion trends. Hip-hop artists frequently wore athletic brands such as Adidas and Nike in the 1980s. As a result, millions of hip-hop fans worldwide began wearing them, too. The skateboarding subculture went even further. They created their own fashion brands such as Thrasher, Vans, and Supreme. While these lines were made specifically for skateboarders at first, they caught on with the general public in the 2010s. Now, these brands are worn by many urban youths, and have become a part of a larger fashion style known as "streetwear."

Brief note

The phrasal verb to *catch on* means to become popular.

Paragraph 4

A person's fashion choices are more than just what's trendy. A person's clothing represents his or her attitudes and values. Since different cultures have different attitudes and values, different brands become popular in different parts of the world. Although marketing influences shoppers' decision making, cultural considerations play a huge part as well. For example, the standard of beauty in East Asia is sometimes described as "softer" or "cuter" than that of Western countries. This makes certain brands and fashion styles less popular in certain areas, while boosting the popularity of others.

2. Talk about the questions after you read and listen.

1. What else influences how people dress?
2. Have you seen any of the fashions or brands mentioned in the passage? What is your opinion of them?
3. What other subcultures have their own clothing styles?
4. What differences are there between fashion in your culture and in other parts of the world?

3. Choose the best title for each paragraph.

________ Regional Differences	________ Why Do Fashion Tastes Differ?
________ When Your Hobby Becomes a Style	________ Dressing Like Your Favorite Star

4. Check the five statements below that are true according to the information in the reading.

1. ☐ "Grunge" fashion helped to define a generation.
2. ☐ Audrey Hepburn designed the first "little black dress."
3. ☐ Kanye West has entered the clothing industry.
4. ☐ People started wearing sports clothing brands in the 1980s because of athletes.
5. ☐ People who were into skateboarding invented their own clothing style.
6. ☐ "Streetwear" is a general style that includes skater fashions.
7. ☐ Marketing is one factor that affects fashion trends.
8. ☐ Ideas of beauty are considered the same in East Asia as in the West.

C Vocabulary

1. Write the words from the box under the correct pictures.

urban	identify	individual	marketing	boost

1. ________ 2. ________ 3. ________ 4. ________ 5. ________

2. Choose the word that is closest in meaning to the word in bold.

1. In some cultures, the color red **represents** passion.

a. becomes b. causes c. means

2. Steve Jobs, one of the founders of Apple, became an **icon** of the tech industry.

a. inventor b. hero c. boss

3. I sometimes borrow clothes from Irina because she and I have similar **tastes**.

a. interests b. preferences c. trends

4. Koreans living abroad have helped to **popularize** Korean food around the world.

a. make known b. make better c. make interesting

5. I was close to my grandfather while growing up, so he had a big **influence** on me.

a. memory b. kindness c. effect

D In Your World

Style and Style Icons

Discuss the questions with a partner.

1. Can you identify these styles? What times, places, and/or subcultures do they represent? Give your opinion of each.

2. Do you have any personal style icons? If so, why did you choose them? How do they influence your style?

WRITING

Each group will discuss one of the topics below. During discussions, someone from each group should be assigned to take notes on the lines below. After discussions, another person from each group can stand up to present their group's results to the class.

Group One: Korean-Style Weddings Are Better than Western-Style Weddings

Group Two: Western-Style Weddings Are Better than Korean-Style Weddings

Group Three: A Mix of Korean and Western Traditions Make the Best Weddings

SUPPLEMENTAL READING

Did Jane Austen Ever Fall in Love?

Track 60

There is not a lot of detailed biographical information available about Jane Austen. This is largely because, after her death at the age of forty-two from Hodgkin's disease in 1817, many of the letters she wrote to friends and loved ones were burned by her family. The letters were probably destroyed to protect Austen's reputation and privacy. The fact that she never married, despite writing so much on the subject of love, has kept fans curious about Austen's romantic experiences.

Though it has never been proven, many suspect that Austen did have at least one passionate love affair during her relatively short life. In 1795, when she was twenty, a young law student from Ireland named Tom Lefroy came to stay with some relatives of his who lived near the Austen family. No one knows exactly how and where he and Jane met, but it is documented that they spent considerable time together. There is also a good chance that they developed feelings for one another.

Sadly, it was not practical for the couple to marry since neither of them had any money. Lefroy was dependent on a wealthy uncle to finance his continued education. Consequently, his family sent him away in January 1796, and he and Jane are not known to have met again. That year, Austen began working on the novel that was eventually published as *Pride and Prejudice* in 1813. Some believe her personal experiences may have influenced the novel's plot, and some critics speculate that Lefroy may have been Austen's model for the character of Darcy.

Fill in the blanks with information from the reading.

1. Austen's family probably burned her letters to protect her ______________________.
2. If Austen and Lefroy did actually want to marry, they couldn't do so because neither had ______________________.
3. Austen began working on her novel ______________________ the same year she and Lefroy apparently ended their relationship.

EXTENSION Talk or Write About It

Can you think of any other books/plays/movies whose creator used his or her own experiences in the story?

UNIT 10-2 Culture

Scan for Audio

Pre-Reading Questions

◆ **Think about the following questions.**

1. Do you like detective stories? Why or why not?
2. Have you read any Sherlock Holmes short stories or novels? If so, what did you think?
3. Who are the most famous fictional characters in your culture? Do you know whether these characters are based on real people?

VOCABULARY PREVIEW

◆ **Match each word with the correct definition.**

1. supposedly	a. a doctor who performs operations
2. accent	b. quick-witted; smart
3. surgeon	c. an applicant or possible choice for a position
4. clever	d. a relationship or connection between two or more things
5. candidate	e. according to a particular source, often unverified
6. correlation	f. a way of pronouncing words that is specific to a certain group

Manchester's Sherlock Holmes

Track 61

Outside 221b Baker Street, London, a **plaque**[1] proclaims Sherlock Holmes once lived there. According to local lore, many foreign tourists visit the site—which happens to be the Sherlock Holmes Museum—apparently unaware that the world's most famous Briton is a fictional character.

In fact, there was no such address when Sir Arthur Conan Doyle wrote his detective stories. (It was added when Baker Street was extended in the 1930s.) And accounts of droves of adoring but **supposedly** ignorant fans are also suspect. But such stories—and the canon of Holmes fiction that expands to this day—speak to the appeal of the character. Now, one author claims, there is evidence Doyle based Holmes on a real police detective: Jerome Caminada, known in his own time as "the Sherlock Holmes of Manchester."

Angela Buckley is the author of the 2014 book *The Real Sherlock Holmes: The Hidden Story of Jerome Caminada*. In it, she examines Manchester detective Caminada's autobiography and Doyle's work to draw comparisons between the real detective—active around the time Doyle created Holmes—and the fictional **sleuth**[2]. "There are so many parallels," she concludes, "that it is clear Doyle was using parts of this real character for his." Chief among these similarities, Buckley asserts, is **intellect**[3]. Doyle's fiction hinged on Holmes' almost superhuman powers of deductive reasoning and observation. Caminada, Buckley reports, could identify a career criminal by his walk and had an "encyclopedic knowledge" of the criminal underworld.

Underline the main similarity between Holmes and Caminada.

As with Holmes, Caminada was a master of disguise. Holmes goes undercover in many stories, as an Italian priest, a sailor, and an opium addict, among many examples. On real cases, Caminada dressed as a drunkard, a laborer, and even an upper-class professional, imitating the **accents** of each in order to gather information and apprehend suspects.

Buckley goes on to draw parallels between Caminada's real cases and the fictional

1	**plaque**	*n.*	a flat, thin piece of wood or metal with writing on it used as reminder of something such as a historic event
2	**sleuth**	*n.*	a detective
3	**intellect**	*n.*	the power of rational or intelligent thought

Circle the names of two other men that might have inspired the character of Holmes.

capers Holmes solves. Like Holmes, she explains, Caminada apprehended an alluring femme fatale and had a brilliant arch-nemesis. The two were also **formidable**[4] fighters in spite of their modest **stature**[5].

Is the case closed? Did Doyle in fact base Holmes on Caminada? Going straight to the source, Doyle very clearly identified the medical professor Dr. Joseph Bell as his inspiration for Holmes. Bell was **renowned**[6] for his keen powers of reasoning in medical diagnoses. Doyle biographers have also suggested development of the character may have been influenced by Sir Henry Littlejohn, an acquaintance who was a forensic **surgeon** with intimate knowledge of hundreds of criminal investigations.

Much of Buckley's premise rests on timing. Caminada had risen to national prominence, she argues, when Doyle was developing Sherlock Holmes. But so had other detectives, such as Leicester's Francis "Tanky" Smith, also known for **clever** disguises and for his vast knowledge of the criminal world. Even if there were only one **candidate** who **fit the bill**[7], this leaves the question of why Doyle would not credit a detective who inspired him, despite being perfectly willing to credit a physician.

What did some police officers resent about Sherlock Holmes stories?

Furthermore, most of Buckley's work is based on **unverified**[8] accounts from Jerome Caminada's autobiography, published fifteen years after the first appearance of Sherlock Holmes. One reviewer has pointed out some contemporary police detectives resented Doyle's portrayals of them as **mediocre**[9]. Did Caminada use his book to show that real police were better than that? We cannot be sure, but it is safe to say he had clear motives to present himself in a flattering light.

This brings us to the modern author and, apparently, the only proponent of the Caminada theory. Although she bills herself as a "family historian," Buckley is, in fact, a **genealogist**[10] and has no academic background in history. She may be faulted for failing to verify claims from a single source—an autobiography at that—and for basing her claims on loose **correlations**. But no one can prove she is wrong, either. The question may be destined to remain a mystery.

Reading Time: _______ minutes _______ seconds 653 words

[4] **formidable**	*adj.*	very powerful or strong; deserving respect
[5] **stature**	*n.*	height
[6] **renowned**	*adj.*	famous
[7] **fit the bill**	*idiom*	to have the required characteristics
[8] **unverified**	*adj.*	not proven or checked for accuracy
[9] **mediocre**	*adj.*	not very good
[10] **genealogist**	*n.*	a person who traces or studies the descent of persons or families

READING COMPREHENSION

A **Mark each statement as true (T) or false (F) according to the reading.**

1. ______ Sherlock Holmes actually lived in the building at 221b Baker Street.
2. ______ Sir Arthur Conan Doyle and Jerome Caminada were real-life rivals.
3. ______ Buckley's book identifies Caminada as a highly intelligent man.
4. ______ Caminada published his autobiography before the first Sherlock Holmes story was written.
5. ______ Buckley's claims have been neither proven nor disproven.

B **Choose the best answer according to the reading.**

1. What is the reading mainly about? TOPIC
   a. The remarkable career of detective Jerome Caminada
   b. An evaluation of the central claims in Angela Buckley's book
   c. The uncanny similarities between a real and a fictional detective
   d. A summary of Sir Arthur Conan Doyle's Sherlock Holmes stories

2. The word *apprehend* in paragraph 4 is closest in meaning to ______. VOCABULARY
   a. understand
   b. notice
   c. escape
   d. catch

3. The phrase *The two* in paragraph 5 refers to ______. REFERENCE
   . Buckley and Doyle
   b. Holmes and Caminada
   c. Holmes and his nemesis
   d. Caminada and his femme fatale

4. Which of the following is NOT stated about Angela Buckley? DETAIL
   a. She has a degree in 19th-century history.
   b. She studies people's family backgrounds.
   c. She is the sole advocate of the Caminada theory.
   d. She has made claims based on one source.

C **Fill in the blanks with information from the reading.**

1. Today 221b Baker Street is the address of the ____________________.
2. ____________________ is the only person Doyle specifically identified as an inspiration for Sherlock Holmes.
3. ____________________ was a Leicester detective who used disguises and knew a lot about criminals.

SUMMARY

Fill in the blanks with the phrases in the box.

disguised himself	knew a surgeon	a genealogist
formidable opponents	deductive reasoning	unverified accounts

Cultural Differences	Biological Differences
• Both Holmes and Caminada had strong powers of 1 ______ and knowledge of criminals. • Holmes 2 ______ to catch criminals, as did Caminada. • Both men had dealings with 3 ______.	• Doyle identified Dr. Joseph Bell as his inspiration and 4 ______ with knowledge of many criminal cases. • Buckley used 5 ______ from an autobiography. • Buckley is 6 ______ rather than a historian.

VOCABULARY PRACTICE

Fill in the blanks with the words in the box. Change the form if necessary.

accent	candidate	clever	correlation	supposedly	surgeon

1. The different regional ______ that people have can tell you which part of the country they are from.
2. The ______ says that her hands are her most important tool.
3. Comedians often have to come up with ______ responses to people who shout at them from the audience.
4. A(n) ______ between a health problem and a certain product does not prove the product is causing the problem.
5. Santa Claus ______ has flying reindeer and can visit every home on Earth in a single night, but that's just not possible.
6. Although there are ten qualified ______, there are only five jobs available.

SPEAKING

10B The Art of Filmmaking

A Authentic Text

Read the blog post.

Traditionally, the word "art" meant "fine art"—that is, creative or visual artworks that meet a high aesthetic standard. The fine arts used to consist of just painting, sculpture, architecture, music, and poetry. However, technology has created new ways to make art. Photography and film are now usually included in the fine arts. But should they be? What makes a film artistic? Also, how can we distinguish between fine art films and popular films?

Film as a fine art is hard to define since it is not just about creating beautiful **images**. Many critics **argue** that certain films, such as *Citizen Kane* and *2001: A Space Odyssey*, are fine art because they contain **complex** meaning. Then there are films which arguably have less **artistic** value, such as *The Fast and the Furious* and the *Transformers* series. These films are made mostly to entertain rather than to deliver meaningful messages. Also, there are films such as *Avatar* and *Star Wars* which were **impressive** because they told entertaining stories and pushed filmmaking to new levels.

What are your thoughts? Express your opinions in the comments below.

Anakinhatessandfan1
Star Wars is a work of art. It popularized science fiction in movies. Science fiction films used to be scary and depressing, but *Star Wars* made them fun. It also created new technologies and ways of looking at filmmaking. As a kid, I would watch it over and over and always notice something new.

GRRForeva97
No, *Star Wars* isn't art. It's a typical hero's tale that stole ideas from more artistic films such as Akira Kurosawa's *Hidden Fortress*. While I was watching it, I was thinking about those better movies the entire time. A lot of people **praise** the special effects, but today, they look ridiculous! *Star Wars* was designed to be a blockbuster, not a work of art.

Brief note

Blockbuster is an informal word for a movie that is extremely popular and makes a lot of money.

B Vocabulary

1. Fill in the blanks with the correct words in bold from the reading.

1. The plot was too __________; it was difficult to understand.
2. Critics always __________ this actress for her smart, funny performances.
3. The film made $50 million, which is a(n) __________ amount for a small, independent movie.
4. Small children shouldn't watch horror movies because the scary __________ upset them.
5. Some people __________ that pop music isn't really art, while others disagree.
6. I don't have any __________ talent, but my brother is an excellent painter.

2. **Match the words with the correct definitions.**

1. aesthetic •	• a. a story, especially an exciting or dramatic one
2. visual •	• b. complete; whole
3. entire •	• c. relating to beauty
4. tale •	• d. to show what you think or how you feel using words or actions
5. meaningful •	• e. relating to seeing or to the eyes
6. distinguish •	• f. the most important idea of a film, book, etc.
7. express •	• g. to notice or identify a difference between people or things
8. message •	• h. having real importance or value

C Grammar

Past tenses; *used to* and *would*

simple past and past continuous	
simple past	**past continuous**
actions completed in the past; things that were true in the past	actions happening at a specific time in the past, and/or that continued for a significant time in the past
Traditionally, the word "art" **meant** "fine art." *Star Wars* **popularized** science fiction. It **stole** ideas from more artistic films.	We **weren't living** here in 2015. What **were** you **doing** at 10 p.m. last night? While I **was watching** that film, I **was thinking** about better movies.
The two tenses are often used together. In these cases, a longer action (described with the past continuous verb) is often interrupted by a quicker action (described with the simple past verb).	
When the director **was filming** the most important scene, the star actor **quit**. The argument **started** when we **were discussing** whether *Star Wars* is a work of art or not. I **was watching** old movies on TV. Then I suddenly **had** a great idea for a script.	

1. **Fill in the blanks with the correct form of the given verbs. Use the simple past or the past continuous.**

   1. The director Akira Kurosawa ________________ (*make*) *Hidden Fortress* in 1958. Critics ________________ (*praise*) it highly, and it ________________ (*do*) well at the box office.
   2. I ________________ (*not see*) the entire movie. It was so complex and boring, I ________________ (*fall*) asleep while I ________________ (*watch*) it.
   3. We ________________ (*start*) arguing when we ________________ (discuss) whether *Star Wars* is a work of art or not.

used to* and *would	
used to	***would***
***Used to* + verb** can describe a past habit, a past repeated action, or a past state. It is used to talk about things that no longer happen or are no longer true.	***Would* + verb** is similar to *used to*. However, it is only used to describe past habits or repeated actions, not states. (It is not normally used with *be* or other stative verbs.)
The fine arts **used to consist** of painting, sculpture, architecture, music, and poetry. Science fiction films **used to be** scary and depressing.	As a kid, I **would watch** it over and over. Back then, each of his films **would make** millions of dollars.

2. **Circle the correct words.**

   1. As a young man, he was very artistic and (would / used to) express himself through photography.
   2. Did Sarah (use to / would) want to become an actress?
   3. I (used to / would) think that romantic comedies were great, but now I can't stand them.

D Use the Language

Is it art?

Brief note

In questions and negative sentences, *use to* (without *-d*) is correct.
Did you **use to** like action movies?
I **didn't use to** like action movies.

1. Think of a hit movie from the past that you enjoyed. Do you think it is a work of art or not? On a separate sheet of paper, write a short paragraph (five to seven sentences) expressing your opinion and giving reasons.
2. Exchange paragraphs with a partner. Read and discuss each other's opinions.

WRITING

1. What foreign music or films are you interested in? What makes them interesting to you?

2. What aspects of Korean culture do you think are the most popular in foreign countries? (ex. K pop, K food, K dramas, etc.)

SUPPLEMENTAL READING

"Peelers" and "Bobbies"

Track 62

The British are generally perceived as a polite and civilized people, especially now that the sun has finally set on the Empire. This is partly a result of Victorian concerns about manners and propriety, which raises the question of what caused those concerns. A look at 18th-century London provides an answer. With no organized police force and with public manners, morals, and a violent-crime rate that were shocking by today's standards, London of this era resembled the Wild West; it was chaos. And this was a problem.

By the early 19th century, Londoners were fed up with crime. In 1829, just two years after Queen Victoria's coronation, the statesman Sir Robert Peel was tasked with establishing London's first organized, citywide police force, with headquarters at Scotland Yard. As he took personal responsibility for their performance, the populace associated officers closely with Robert (or "Bob" for short) Peel. Hence the terms "Peelers" and "Bobbies"—slang for police officers in Ireland and England, respectively.

Peel's police force was based on successful military units with civil-policing duties. And Peel introduced several concepts that are central to modern policing. These "Peelian Principles" essentially established the "serve and protect" standard. Peel believed a police force should maintain law and order, but in service of the public and with their consent and cooperation. The use of force was a last resort, and Peel expected his men to earn respect through devotion to duty and proper conduct. By all accounts, the Bobbies did indeed help restore order. And although much has changed in policing, the basic call to protect citizens rather than control them remains central to the mission of the department to this day.

Fill in the blanks with information from the reading.

1. London in the 18th century had a shockingly high rate of ______________________________.
2. "Peelers" is the slang word for police officers in ______________________________.
3. The "Peelian Principles" mean that police should maintain law and order with the public's ______________________________.

EXTENSION Talk or Write About It

Why do you think Sherlock Holmes is such a popular character? How are police and/or private detectives viewed in your country?

MEMO